Ramadhān with The Holy Qur'ān

30 Lessons in 30 days

Ayatullah Mohsen Qarāti

Lantern Publications
info@lanternpublications.com
www.lanternpublications.com

Ordering Information:

Quantity sales. Special discounts are available on quantity purchases by corporations, associations, and others. For details, contact the distributor at the address below.

Shia Books Australia
www.shiabooks.com.au
info@shiabooks.com.au

ISBN-978-600-5421-36-1

Second Edition 2023

A catalogue record for this book is available from the National Library of Australia

For information on Hujjat Al Islam **Mohsen Qarāti**, please visit http://gharaati.ir/

In the Name of God,
the Most Compassionate, the Most Merciful

Prayers of God's Peace and Blessings

In keeping with the Islamic practice of showing respect for the name of God, and sending prayers of God's peace and blessings whenever the name of His blessed Prophet, Lady Fātima, and the Twelve Imams is mentioned, as well as for asking God to hasten the reappearance of the Lord of the Age on the Earthly plane, one or more of the following Arabic symbols have been employed throughout the text.

Used exclusively after the name of God, meaning "the Sublimely Exalted", or, as a prayer, "[May His name be] Sublimely Exalted".

Used exclusively after the name of the Prophet Mohammad, meaning "May the peace and blessings of God be unto him and unto [the purified and inerrant members of] his family" (i.e. Lady Fātima and the Twelve Imams).

Used for any of the Twelve Imams or past prophets of God, meaning "May God's peace be unto him".

Used for two or more of the Twelve Imams or past prophets of God, meaning "May God's peace be unto them".

Used for Lady Fātima, meaning "May God's peace be unto her".

Used for a plurality of the Fourteen Immaculates (the Prophet Mohammad, Lady Fātima, and the Twelve Imams), meaning "May God's peace be unto them all collectively".

Used for the Master of the Age (the Twelfth Imam), meaning "May God hasten the advent of his noble person".

Authors note

In the Name of God, the Most Merciful, the Most Compassionate. All Praise Is to Allah The Sustainer of The Worlds, And May Allahs' Blessings Be Upon Muhammad And His Purified Household.

Dear Reader

Peace Be Upon You

In the Holy Month of Ramadhān, 1392[1], a group of friends came up with the idea of a small booklet be produced for the Qur'ānic Competition that was small, easy to read and understand based on the Exegesis of Noor with some alterations as needed.

The thirty lessons of this booklet, Ramadhān with The Holy Qur'ān, has been produced from the words of the Holy Qur'ān and exegesis as well as points from traditions and narrations from the Divine Purified Household. We hope that the choices made, and summary produced is a step towards being more familiar with the Holy Qur'ān and Narrations and be a means of saving your precious time in this fast-paced world.

We wish you all, that Allah accepts your sincerity and gives you blessings and accepts your worship and efforts in the Holy Month of Ramadhān and all other months and hope these lines and efforts are appreciated and we ask from all, for I am in need of it, your prayers and supplications.

Mohsen Qarāti

---

[1] July/August 2013

Translators Note

Thanks to the All-Mighty Lord and praise and blessings to the Prophet❋ and his Pure Progeny peace be upon them… and may the return of Imam Al-Mahdi ❋ – Our Saviour, be hastened in this troubled world, for surely, the time for his return is soon, although the enemy sees it as far.

Forgiveness is sought for any shortcomings in the translation of this work, firstly from the Merciful Allah❋, from the Prophet' and from his Pure Progeny … and from the author of the work.

This translation is, first and foremost, dedicated to Sayyida Fāṭima *Masūma, Peace and Blessings Upon Her.*

My father and mother, whose unwavering support keeps me strong, as well as my brother and sister, and my wife for overviewing the translation.

After over a year of working slowly but surely, this translation has finally come to an end as the second translation of a series of booklets published by the author. His works are easy to understand and answer some complex questions in a simple manner, bringing to light to the youth the essence of faith in a bite sized format that's easy to swallow.

We hope this translation reflects those efforts, and we ask for your prayers.

S.L. Al-Hakim
30th April 2017

Contents

Lesson 1- Ramadhān

A Month Hosted by Allah

شَهْرُ رَمَضَانَ ٱلَّذِىٓ أُنزِلَ فِيهِ ٱلْقُرْءَانُ هُدًى لِّلنَّاسِ وَبَيِّنَٰتٍ مِّنَ ٱلْهُدَىٰ وَٱلْفُرْقَانِ فَمَن شَهِدَ مِنكُمُ ٱلشَّهْرَ فَلْيَصُمْهُ وَمَن كَانَ مَرِيضًا أَوْ عَلَىٰ سَفَرٍ فَعِدَّةٌ مِّنْ أَيَّامٍ أُخَرَ يُرِيدُ ٱللَّهُ بِكُمُ ٱلْيُسْرَ وَلَا يُرِيدُ بِكُمُ ٱلْعُسْرَ وَلِتُكْمِلُوا ٱلْعِدَّةَ وَلِتُكَبِّرُوا ٱللَّهَ عَلَىٰ مَا هَدَىٰكُمْ وَلَعَلَّكُمْ تَشْكُرُونَ

"The month of Ramadhān, wherein the Holy Qur'ān was sent down to be a guidance to the people, and as clear signs of the Guidance and the Salvation. So let those of you, who are present at the month, fast it; and if any of you be sick, or if he be on a journey, then a number of other days; God desires ease for you, and desires not hardship for you; and that you fulfil the number, and magnify God that He has guided you, and haply you will be thankful." – Surah Al Baqarah 2:185.

Ramadhān is a word that comes from the root word "رَمض" which means to burn, but a burning which is not accompanied by smoke and ash. The reason for this name is that in the month of Ramadhān, the sins of mankind are burnt and destroyed.

The month of Ramadhān is the month in which the Holy Qur'ān was sent down and is the only month that has been named in the Holy Qur'ān. The Night of Qadr (commonly translated to the Night of Power) is also in this month. The Prophet ﷺ said that "All of the divine books were sent down during the month of Ramadhān, the best of Allah's ❀ months".[1] On the last Friday in the month of Sha'bān (the month before Ramadhān), a detailed sermon was delivered by the Prophet ﷺ regarding the significance of the month of Ramadhān which is made available to us through some of the commentaries of the Holy Qur'ān and through books of narrations. Furthermore, in the Sahifa Sajjādiya, Imam Sajjād ﷜ greets this Holy Month with a supplication and farewells it with a heart wrenching supplication.

In Ramadhān, believers are invited as guests to be hosted by Allah❀ with the following Ayah of the Qur'ān:

يَا أَيُّهَا الَّذِينَ آمَنُوا كُتِبَ عَلَيْكُمُ الصِّيَامُ كَمَا كُتِبَ عَلَى الَّذِينَ مِن قَبْلِكُمْ لَعَلَّكُمْ تَتَّقُونَ

O believers, prescribed for you is the Fast, even as it was prescribed for those that were before you --so perhaps you will be godfearing – Surah Al Baqarah 2:183

This invitation has the following special characteristics:

1. The host is Allah❀ and the guests have been personally invited.
2. The reception is made up of the Night of Qadr, the sending of the Holy Qur'ān, the decending of the Angels, the answers to supplications, the beneficence of the soul, and to be distanced from the Hell-fire.
3. The time and duration of the reception is the month of Ramadhān, which according to narrations, the first of which is mercy, the middle of which is forgiveness, and the conclusion of which is reward.
4. The way the guests are greeted in the Night of Power, guarantees ones provisions for guests for one year and the earth is decorated with the descending of the Angels to it.
5. The food served in this month is nutrition for the soul which is needed for spiritual growth, not food for the body. The benefit of the food of this month, which are the Ayāt of the Holy Qur'ān for which the recitation of one Ayah in the month of Ramadhān, is equivalent to the recitation of the entire Holy Qur'ān during other months.

This invitation cannot be compared to or be likened to any worldly invitation; the All Knowledgeable, Needless, Creator, Everlasting, Beloved, Exalted, is

---

[1] (Al Burhan - البرهان فى تفسير القرآن)

the host for mankind who are ignorant, poor, perishable, created, servile and needy.

In Wasa'il Al Sh'ia[1], in detailed narrations of the characteristics of a fasting person, we read "*A fasting person must avoid lying, sin, dispute, jealousy, back biting, opposing the truth, swearing, blaming, anger, sarcasm, oppression, abusing people, neglect, being social with those who sin, slander and gossip, eating non-permissible things, while paying special attention with regards to prayers, patience, truthfulness and being in constant remembrance of the Day of Resurrection*".

Conditions of entry into the reception is not only the withstanding of hunger. We read in narrations that anyone who does not obey the Divine Guide in relation to personal and family matters, behaves badly and without mercy with their spouse, and/or refuses legitimate means of obtaining their needs or wants, and/or if the parents are not happy with them, the fasting of that person is not accepted nor have the conditions of being a guest been fulfilled.

The value of Ramadhān is with the descending of the Holy Qur'ān. The worth of the human can also come with some penetration of the Holy Qur'ān inside them.

The Sermon of Sha'bān

Imam Ali ؏ narrates that the Prophet ﷺ, on the last Friday of Sha'bān[2], gave a speech in which after he Praised Allah ﷻ, he stated[3]:

"O People !

"Indeed, ahead of you is the blessed month of Allah. A month of blessing, mercy, and forgiveness. A month which with Allah is the best of months. Its days, the best of days, its nights, the best of nights, and its hours, the best of hours. It is the month which invites you to be the guests of Allah and invites you to be one of those near to Him. Each breath you take glorifies him; your sleep is worship; your deeds are accepted, and your supplications are answered.

---

[1] (Wasa'il Al Shia وسائل الشيعة)

[2] The lunar month just before the Holy Month of Ramadhān.

[3] Translation compliments of Al-Islam.org, Supplications for the Month of Ramadhān. Available from http://www.al-islam.org/supplications-month-Ramadhān/sermon-given-prophet-s-last-friday-shaban-reception-month-Ramadhān, date cited 01/02/16.

So, ask Allah, your Lord; to give you a sound body and an enlightened heart so you may be able to fast and recite his book, for only he is unhappy who is devoid of Allah's forgiveness during this great month. Remember the hunger and thirst of the day of Qiyamah (Judgement) with your hunger and thirst; give alms to the needy and poor, honour your old, show kindness to the young ones, maintain relations with your blood relations; guard your tongues, close your eyes to that which is not permissible for your sight, close your ears to that which is forbidden to hear, show compassion to the orphans of people so compassion may be shown to your orphans.

Repent to Allah for your sins and raise your hands in du'a during these times, for they are the best of times and Allah looks towards his creatures with kindness, replying to them during the hours and granting their needs if He is asked...

"O People! Indeed, your souls are dependent on your deeds, free it with Istighfār (repentance) lighten its loads by long prostrations; and know that Allah swears by his might: That there is no punishment for the one who prays and prostrates, and he shall have no fear of the fire on the day when man stands before the Lord of the worlds.

"O People! One who gives Iftār to a fasting person during this month will be like one who has freed someone, and his past sins will be forgiven.

Some of the people who were there then asked the Prophet (s): "Not all of us are able to invite those who are fasting?"

The Prophet (s) replied: "Allah gives this reward even if the Iftār (meal) is a drink of water."

"One who has good morals (Akhlāq) during this month will be able to pass the 'Sirāt'...on the day that feet will slip...

"One who covers the faults of others will benefit in that Allah will curb His anger on the day of Judgement...

"As for one who honours an orphan; Allah will honour him on the day of judgement,

"And for the one who spreads his kindness, Allah will spread His mercy over him on the day of Judgement.

"As for the one who cuts the ties of relation; Allah will cut His mercy from him...

"Who so ever performs a recommended prayer in this month Allah will keep the fire of Hell away from him...

"Whoever performs an obligatory prayer Allah will reward him with seventy prayers [worth] in this month.

"And who so ever prays a lot during this month will have his load lightened on the day of measure.

"He who recites one verse of the Holy Qur'ān will be given the rewards of reciting the hole Holy Qur'ān during other months.

"O People! Indeed during this month, the doors of heaven are open, therefore ask Allah not to close them for you; The doors of hell are closed, so ask Allah to keep them closed for you. During this month Shaytān (Satan) is imprisoned so ask your Lord not to let him have power over you."

Imam Ali then asked the Prophet what the best deed is for this Holy Month? To which the Prophet replied – "Oh Abu Al-Hasan, the best deed is Taqwa (the love of and fear from Allah) and abstaining from that which has been forbidden by Him."   After his response, the Prophet started crying, and when Imam Ali asked why… the Prophet replied: "Oh Ali, I can see what will happen to you during this Holy Month, while you pray, the most wretched will strike you on the head and your beard will be coloured by the blood of your head." Imam Ali asked if his religion at that point will be protected?

أفي سلامةٍ من ديني؟

The Prophet replied affirmatively, adding:

"Oh Ali, whoever kills you will have killed me, and whoever angers you will have angered me, and whoever becomes your enemy will have become my enemy. That's because you are from me, your soul is from my soul and your presence is from my presence".

Of course, we must monitor ourselves to be sure to supplicate, worship in an appropriate manner and without causing a racket, nor be ill mannered towards family and friends or be wasteful or extravagant, unjust as guests and during the iftār (after a long day fast), so that not only will we not reap any rewards from our fast but we will have committed a heavier sin.

Lesson 2 Fasting

Effects and Blessings of Fasting

يَا أَيُّهَا الَّذِينَ آمَنُوا كُتِبَ عَلَيْكُمُ الصِّيَامُ كَمَا كُتِبَ عَلَى الَّذِينَ مِن قَبْلِكُمْ لَعَلَّكُمْ تَتَّقُونَ

O believers, prescribed for you is the Fast, even as it was prescribed for those that were before you – so that you will be god-fearing (Al Baqarah 2:183).

"Taqwa" is with the meaning of holding yourself back from sin. Most sins originate from two sources; anger and desire, and fasting controls those two instincts and so reduces corruption and adds to "Taqwa".

God consciousness and the fear of God, or Taqwa, is the most important externally apparent and internally hidden result of fasting.

Fasting is the sole worship which can go unnoticed and hidden from others. Prayer, pilgrimage, Jihad (religious struggle), Islamic Tax (Zakāt)[1] and khums[2] can all be seen by others, but fasting is not something that can be seen. Fasting strengthens the will of human beings.

Someone, who for one month can refrain from bread and water and their spouse, can control themselves with respect to the property and chastity of others. Fasting is the cause of strengthening the feeling of kindness.

---

[1] Islamic Tax

[2] Religiously compulsory charity on earnings in excess of one's necessary expenditure.

Someone, who for one month has tasted hunger and thirst, can feel the pain and understand the difficulty and struggle of hunger.

The Prophet stated that fasting is half of patience.

The fasting of the general population is that of the abstaining of bread, drink, and spouse. However, amongst the more noble, along with the abstinence of the items which break a fast, it is necessary to abstain from sin. The fast of those who are the noblest of the noble is not only abstinence of the items which break a fast, abstinence from sin, but also emptying the heart from everything but Allah. Fasting makes people like angels, angels that are far off from eating, drinking, and desires.

The Prophet' stated that anyone who fasts for the sake of Allah, their entire sins will be forgiven. In the Holy Narration it is also stated that Allah stated

الصوم لي وأنا أجزي به

Fasting is for Me and I will reward for it.[1]

The importance of fasting is so vast, that many of the rewards of worship in the narrations are equated to the reward of observing fast. Although fasting was also prescribed for many nations before, the fasting of the Month of Ramadhān was specific to Prophets, and only became obligatory upon all with the advent of Islam.

It has been narrated from the Prophet that he stated that for everything there is an Islamic Tax (Zakāt), and the Islamic Tax (Zakāt) of the body is fasting.[2]

Etiquette and Conditions of Observing the Fast

أَيَّامًا مَّعْدُودَاتٍ فَمَن كَانَ مِنكُم مَّرِيضًا أَوْ عَلَى سَفَرٍ فَعِدَّةٌ مِّنْ أَيَّامٍ أُخَرَ وَ عَلَى الَّذِينَ يُطِيقُونَهُ فِدْيَةٌ طَعَامُ مِسْكِينٍ فَمَن تَطَوَّعَ خَيْراً فَهُوَ خَيْرٌ لَّهُ وَ أَن تَصُومُواْ خَيْرٌ لَّكُمْ إِن كُنتُمْ تَعْلَمُونَ

for days numbered; and if any of you be sick, or if he be on a journey, then a number of other days; and for those who are not able to fast, a redemption by

---

[1] (Tafsir Maraghi – تفسير المراغي)
[2] (Bihar Al Anwar بحار الأنوار) V60 P380

feeding a poor man. Yet better it is for him who volunteers good, and that you should fast is better for you, if you but know. (Al Baqarah 2:184)

Islam has a suitable law for every person and under every condition. In this Ayah, the law for those who are travelling, or are ill, and are able bodied have been clarified. If under certain conditions one is unable to fast, they must compensate for that fast on another occasion so that they may enjoy the benefits of fasting.

Surrendering to the Divine Laws has its merit. If the rule of observing fast is given, a fast must be observed and if the command is to break the fast, the fast must be broken. In Tafsir Majma' Al Bayan (مجمع البيان في تفسير القرآن), it has been narrated that a group of the companions of the Prophet ﷺ maintained their fast while travelling and did not desire to break it. The Prophet ﷺ identified them as sinners. Imam Sādiq؏ stated that if someone observes a fast during travel, I will not be praying upon his body the prayer of the deceased[1].

In any case, if the traveler or the sick observes a fast it is considered void and it must be compensated for later.[2]

Imam Sādiq؏ stated, even if the mother is concerned about her breastmilk for her child, she must break her fast and this is a symbol of the kindness of Allah﷽.[3]

Breaking The Fast

The Prophet' stated that anyone who provides for others food or water to break the fast (after fasting) purchased with halal income, will have praise sent for them every hour by angels and on the Night of Power by Archangel Jibrael ؏.[4]

Breaking the fast is one form of worship provided it is with purity and intention is solely for nearness to Allah﷽.

---

[1] Similar to requiem prayer. i.e. he has disobeyed Allah to the extent of not deserving of this fundamental right every Muslim enjoys.

[2] (Tafsīr Nūr al-Thaqalayn - تفسير نور الثقلين)

[3] (Al Burhan - البرهان فى تفسير القرآن)- Please refer to your Mar'ja regarding the rule for your circumstance.

[4] (Kanz Ul Amal - كنز العمال) V8 P459

إِنَّمَا نُطْعِمُكُمْ لِوَجْهِ اللَّهِ

We feed you only for the sake of God. (Al Insān 76:9)

Providing iftaar to believers according to Imam Sādiq is like the Night Prayer which is a cause of salvation and prosperity.

المنجيات إطعام الطعام

Providing iftaar is a kind of honour and instilling happiness to believers.

Providing iftaar is a cause for softening of the heart, maintaining familial relations, cause for the removal of grudges and hypocrisy.

Providing iftaar is a source of forgiveness for oneself and family, and source of benefit and goodness to parents.

Providing iftaar is a vehicle for invitation and showing the right path and guidance.

The aim of providing iftaar must not be showing off.

The invitation to iftaar must not be only for the rich and those with status and position.

The dining table must not be one of crime or sin or despise and backbiting or provocation.

It must not be disrespectful and mannerless, and the guests should not be greeted with contempt.

It must not be so decorated and beautified, vying with each other, and competing, nor be conducted with jealousy.

It must not be accompanied with illogical remarks and harassment of the spouse, family and others.

It is narrated that the reward of one who provides iftaar to those who have observed the fast.

Lesson 3 Contemplation in The Holy Qur'ān

Complaint from The Forlorn Holy Qur'ān

وَقَالَ الرَّسُولُ يَا رَبِّ إِنَّ قَوْمِى اتَّخَذُوا هَـٰذَا الْقُرْآنَ مَهْجُورًا

The Messenger says, 'O my Lord, behold, my people have taken this Holy Qur'ān
as a thing to be shunned.' (Furqān, 25:30)

"Forlorn" or "Shun" includes the separation by deed, body, tongue, and heart. So, the connection of man with the Heavenly Book must be constant and under all circumstances, that's why the term "Hijr", translated as shunning, is used where there is a connection between a thing and mankind. Therefore, we must struggle from all angles until the Holy Qur'ān is brought out of the state of being shunned and is made to be the pivotal point of all dimensions of our practical and scientific life until such time as the satisfaction of the Prophet ﷺ is attained.

Not reciting the Holy Qur'ān, preferring anything but the Holy Qur'ān, not using it as our pivot, not contemplating in it, not teaching it to others and not applying the Holy Qur'ān in practice, form the evidence of the shunning of the Holy Qur'ān. Even if someone acquires the Holy Qur'ān but then puts it aside and does not look at it nor commit to it, is another form and evidence of shunning the Holy Qur'ān.

This Ayah is a statement of great sorrow and distress from the Prophet ﷺ because he is a mercy to all the worlds, he would therefore not curse. Yet on the day of judgement the Prophet ﷺ will be one of those complaining against us. And so, the shunning of the Holy Qur'ān, the great sorrow of the Prophet ﷺ and our responsibility is definite and simply reading the Holy Qur'ān on the surface of it is not enough, but rather what is required is bring the Holy Qur'ān out of this state.

Imam Rīḍa ﷺ states, the reason we recite the Holy Qur'ān in our daily prayers is to bring the Holy Qur'ān out of the state of being shunned.

He also advises us to recite fifty Ayāt of the Holy Qur'ān every day and our aim should not be to simply reach the end of the Surah; we should read with tranquillity with our hearts taking refuge in the recitation of the Holy Qur'ān. And whenever our hearts are troubled, such as in the darkness of the night, or we are attacked, we should take shelter with the Holy Qur'ān.[1]

Here, we narrate some of the commentaries by the great scholars on the issue of the forlorn Holy Qur'ān:

A) Mulla Sadra, in his introduction to the commentary on Surah Al-Wāqia'a (Surah 56), says; "So much research was conducted into books written by sages that I was of the opinion that I became somebody [to be worthy of a high intellectual status], however, after just a little insight, I saw myself as empty of true knowledge. Towards the end of my life my thoughts went towards contemplation of the Holy Qur'ān and the narrations of Mohammad ﷺ and his Purified Household ﷺ. I was certain that my work was baseless, as my whole life was spent standing in the shadows instead of in the light. From sorrow, my soul caught on fire and my heart was in flames, until the Divine Mercy caught my hand and lead me to the secrets of the Holy Qur'ān and I started contemplating and commentating on the Holy Qur'ān, I knocked hard on the door of the house of inspiration, the door opened and the curtain moved aside and I saw the angels say to

---

[1] (Tafsīr Nūr al-Thaqalayn - تفسير نور الثقلين)

me "Peace be upon you all, you have all been blessed, so enter it for eternity"."

B) Faydh Kāshāni said: "I have written books and letters, I have researched, yet I have not found a single cure for the pain I have and found the water for my thirst to be evasive, I feared for myself and ran towards Allah؟, begging for guidance through in depth understanding of the Holy Qur'ān and narrations."

C) Imam Khomeini showed regret in one of his speeches for not spending his entire life in the way of the Holy Qur'ān and advised Islamic Seminaries and students to place the Holy Qur'ān in all of its dimensions as the highest goal to head towards lest the end of our life be met with regret with regards to how our youth was spent.

The Necessity for Contemplation In The Holy Qur'ān

كِتَابٌ أَنزَلْنَاهُ إِلَيْكَ مُبَارَكٌ لِيَدَّبَّرُوا آيَاتِهِ وَلِيَتَذَكَّرَ أُولُو الْأَلْبَابِ

A Book We have sent down to thee, Blessed, that men possessed of minds may ponder its signs and so remember. (Sād 38:29)

The image of the Holy Qur'ān in this Ayah has been drawn in the following way:

a) The text of it has been written - كِتَابٌ (A Book).
b) Sourced from the Divine Revelation and Infinite Knowledge - أَنزَلْنَاهُ (We have sent down).
c) The recipient is Divinely Guided – إِلَيْكَ (to thee).
d) Its content is full of blessing – مُبَارَكٌ (blessed).
e) The aim of it being sent is to contemplate – لِيَدَّبَّرُوا (may ponder).
f) Knowledge, awareness and to learn the points with in it are necessary first steps in the spiritual journey and being closer towards Allah؟ – وَلِيَتَذَكَّرَ (and so remember).
g) Wise is the one who succeeds in achieving this.

Therefore, contemplation in the Holy Qur'ān is of the highest significance, because: One who does not contemplate the Ayāt of the Holy Qur'ān is deserving of Divine humiliation.

أَفَلَا يَتَدَبَّرُونَ الْقُرْآنَ أَمْ عَلَىٰ قُلُوبٍ أَقْفَالُهَا

What, do they not ponder the Holy Qur'ān? Or is it that there are locks upon their

hearts? (Muḥammad 47:24)

From the point of view of the Qur'ān, a spiritual scholar is someone whose concern is to learn and teach the Qur'ān.

{كُونُوا رَبَّانِيِّينَ بِمَا كُنتُمْ تُعَلِّمُونَ الْكِتَابَ وَبِمَا كُنتُمْ تَدْرُسُونَ}

Be you masters in that you know the Book, and in that you study (Āle Imrān

3:79).

Imam Ali ﷺ, with regards to the infinite concepts and lessons of the Holy Qur'ān, states بحر لا يدرك قعره

The Holy Qur'ān is a sea for which its bottom can never by understood.

Usually, over a period of time, the sayings and writings of an individual changes and evolves and contradictions may occur. However, over 23 years of revelation, under a multitude of circumstances such as war and peace, fame and exile, strength and weakness, ups and downs, from one who himself was never taught [by any other human], there was never a contradiction nor any evolution or change. The reason being that these words are from Allah and not taught by mankind. So the Holy Qur'ān cautions:

أَفَلَا يَتَدَبَّرُونَ الْقُرْآنَ وَلَوْ كَانَ مِنْ عِندِ غَيْرِ اللَّـهِ لَوَجَدُوا فِيهِ اخْتِلَافًا كَثِيرًا

What, do they not ponder the Holy Qur'ān? If it had been from other than God

surely, they would have found in it much inconsistency. (An Nisā 4:82)

Why is it the Holy Qur'ān is not contemplated over? Where had it been from a source other than from Allah, there would have certainly been many contradictions.

The order to contemplate over the Holy Qur'ān is for everyone and for every era and generation, clear through the fact that every thinker from every era, will arrive at new points from it.

With a little attention on the Ayah, we can benefit from some beautiful points:

1. Not thinking in the Holy Qur'ān is a cause for Divine reproach and taunt.
2. Contemplation in the Holy Qur'ān is a curative medicine for hypocrisy.
3. The way to Islamic orientation and Holy Qur'ān is to think and contemplate, not simply imitate.
4. The Holy Qur'ān has called for all to contemplate and to understand the lessons being taught in it.
5. The thought that within the Holy Qur'ān there are contradictions and differences are a result of shallow anxiety and lack of contemplation and attention to detail.
6. The fact is that there are no contradictions within the Holy Qur'ān and the single voice in which the Holy Qur'ān is said, is a sign that its source is one that is not changeable. This is because anything that is from Allahﷻ is the Truth and is Constant and is far from any contradiction, contrast and possibility of being scattered.

Lesson 4 Points About The Qur'ān

إِنَّا أَنزَلْنَاهُ فِي لَيْلَةٍ مُّبَارَكَةٍ إِنَّا كُنَّا مُنذِرِينَ

We have sent it down in a blessed night. Indeed, We were to warn [mankind]

(Ad Dukhān 44:3).

The Holy Qur'ān is blessed from all aspects. From the point of view of:

1. Who sent it down: تَبَارَكَ الَّذِي نَزَّلَ الْفُرْقَانَ (Blessed be He who has sent down the Salvation. Furqān 25:1).
2. Where it was sent down: بِبَكَّةَ مُبَارَكًا (at Bakka, a holy place. Āle Imrān 3:96).
3. When it was sent down: فِي لَيْلَةٍ مُّبَارَكَةٍ (in a blessed night. Dukhān 44:3).
4. Its content and text: كِتَابٌ أَنزَلْنَاهُ إِلَيْكَ مُبَارَكٌ (A Book We have sent down to thee, Blessed. Sād 38:29).

A Book with Dignity

إِنَّهُ لَقُرْآنٌ كَرِيمٌ فِي كِتَابٍ مَّكْنُونٍ لَّا يَمَسُّهُ إِلَّا الْمُطَهَّرُونَ تَنزِيلٌ مِّن رَّبِّ الْعَالَمِينَ

It is surely a noble Holy Qur'ān, in a hidden Book, none but the purified shall

touch, a sending down from the Lord of all Being. (Wāqi'a 56:77-80).

In the Qur'ān, Allah and anything associated with it is described as كريم which means "with dignity, generous, kind, noble, honourable etc".

1. The Lord is generous: يَا أَيُّهَا الْإِنسَانُ مَا غَرَّكَ بِرَبِّكَ الْكَرِيمِ (O Man! What deceived thee as to thy generous Lord. Infitār 82:6).
2. The Holy Qur'ān is noble: إِنَّهُ لَقُرْآنٌ كَرِيمٌ. (Wāqi'a 56:77).
3. The Messenger is noble: وَجَاءَهُمْ رَسُولٌ كَرِيمٌ (and a noble Messenger came unto them. Dukhān 44:17).
4. The medium in which the Holy Qur'ān was sent through, (Archangel Jibraīl), is noble:

$$\{إِنَّهُ لَقَوْلُ رَسُولٍ كَرِيمٍ\}$$

Truly this is the word of a noble Messenger.

(Takwīr 81:19).

The human being is also addressed as the best of God's creation, a recipient of nobility.

$$لقد كرمنا بنى آدم$$

We have honoured the sons of Adam (Al Isrā 17:70).

And Imam Ali in speech number 152 of Nahjul Balagha, states the Purified Household are the dignitaries of the Qur'ān.

$$كرائم القرآن$$

Yes, the Holy Qur'ān is the key to honour and nobility of an individual and society. Looking at it, reciting it and memorising it (with preservation), contemplating in it and seeking advice from it, is a source of growth and honour for mankind. For it is certainly a Noble Qur'ān.

Some of the distinctions this infinitely and everlasting miraculous Holy Qur'ān have been described in Tafsīr Nūr under Ayah 38 of Surah Yunus as follows:

1. The assertion of big lessons in small words: For example, with regards to man and women, the Holy Qur'ān states

هُنَّ لِبَاسٌ لَّكُمْ وَأَنتُمْ لِبَاسٌ لَّهُنَّ

They are a vestment for you, and you are a vestment for them. (Al Baqarah 2:187).

And to indicate the weakness of everything other than that of Divine Strength, it uses the simile of the spiders' house. Or like the inability of anyone to be able to create even a single fly:

لَن يَخْلُقُوا ذُبَابًا

Shall never create a fly (Al Ḥajj 22:73).

2. The sweetness of the statements and its profound influence: Even if read a thousand times over, it never grows old, on the contrary, every time it is read, new guidance can be obtained.
3. The melodious tone of the words: The reverberations and the tone of the words is unique and if an Ayah of the Holy Qur'ān is stated amongst a speech or among narrations, the Ayah stands out being is easily identifiable.
4. The comprehensiveness of the Qur'ān: With in the Holy Qur'ān there is everything from clear evidence through to parables, from this world to the afterlife, from issues of family, rights, political, military, through to morality, history and more…
5. Its realities: The contents of the Holy Qur'ān are not based upon guesswork and opinion. Even its stories are based on realities.
6. For all obstacles and conditions: People of all classes and in all places can take benefit from it and the Holy Qur'ān is not a specialised book.
7. Everlasting and eternal: The more that one's life passes, and knowledge is gained, more of the secrets of the Holy Qur'ān are revealed.
8. Stimulant for growth: Despite having many enemies and having been attacked so much, it has grown stronger throughout its life.
9. A miracle in the hand: This is a miracle that is in the hands of all and is the kind of literature that is available to everyone.
10. It is a book of preaching as well as a book of laws and regulations.
11. It has come from one who did not study and from an area that was deprived of literacy.

31

12. Nothing has been added to it nor anything taken away from it and is immune from all alteration.
13. The source of healing and mercy. The Doctor of this medicine not only knows us, but also loves us and the result of the prescription is eternal, without any parallel or anything like it.

The Miracle of The Holy Qur'ān

أَمْ يَقُولُونَ افْتَرَاهُ قُلْ فَأْتُوا بِعَشْرِ سُوَرٍ مِّثْلِهِ مُفْتَرَيَاتٍ وَادْعُوا مَنِ اسْتَطَعْتُم مِّن دُونِ اللَّـهِ إِن كُنتُمْ صَادِقِينَ

Or they may say, "He forged it," Say, "Bring ye then ten surahs forged, like unto it, and call (to your aid) whomsoever ye can, other than Allah! - If ye speak the truth!

(Hūd 11:13)

The Holy Qur'ān is not only a miracle with regards to its eloquence and its delivery of the message, but also is its lessons, sermons, proofs, news of the unseen and its laws are all miracles, and so the sentence:

وَادْعُوا مَنِ اسْتَطَعْتُم

and call (to your aid) anyone you can...

is a call to all of mankind, not only to the Arabs who understand the eloquence and the message of the Holy Qur'ān. Likewise, in another Ayah the Holy Qur'ān states:

قُل لَّئِنِ اجْتَمَعَتِ الْإِنسُ وَالْجِنُّ عَلَىٰ أَن يَأْتُوا بِمِثْلِ هَـٰذَا الْقُرْآنِ لَا يَأْتُونَ بِمِثْلِهِ وَلَوْ كَانَ بَعْضُهُمْ لِبَعْضٍ ظَهِيرًا

Say: "If the whole of mankind and Jinn were to gather together to produce the like of this Qur'ān, they could not produce the like thereof, even if they backed up each other with help and support. (Al-Isrā 17:88)

There are many sides to the miracles of the Qur'ān: the pleasance and sweetness of the recitation of the words, the uniformity of its content despite its revelation over 23 years, the exposition of scientific facts that were until that time unknown to mankind, the foretelling of events that letter occurred, news of civilization in history long gone that no longer have any traces left behind, the delivery of complete and comprehensive instructions in all aspects of individual and social life of mankind, remaining far from any form of distortion, any change, aging, and the continuation of the guarantee against it being forgotten.

But with all the concessions and all the incentives, mankind remains feeble. In one place the Holy Qur'ān states

أَن يَأْتُوا بِمِثْلِ هَـٰذَا الْقُرْآنِ

To gather together to produce the like of this Holy Qur'ān (Al-Isrā 17:88)

And in another Ayah, it eases the challenge to producing just ten Ayāt like that of the Qur'ān, and elsewhere, a further easing to just one Surah:

فَأْتُوا بِسُورَةٍ مِّن مِّثْلِهِ

Then produce a Surah like thereunto (Al Baqarah 2:23).

In addition to reducing these challenges, there are also various instigations included. Such as the Ayah that states even if all the men and Jinn come together, they cannot meet the challenge. And elsewhere, summon all the mind power on earth, and you all can still not produce anything like the Qur'ān.

History has proven that despite all the wars by the enemies against Islam, and with all the conspiracies, they have not been able to bring a single surah like that of the Qur'ān. Is a miracle anything other than this?

The Distinction of Qur'ānic Stories

نَحْنُ نَقُصُّ عَلَيْكَ أَحْسَنَ الْقَصَصِ بِمَا أَوْحَيْنَا إِلَيْكَ هَـٰذَا الْقُرْآنَ وَإِن كُنتَ مِن قَبْلِهِ لَمِنَ الْغَافِلِينَ

We will relate to thee the best of stories in that We have revealed to thee this Holy Qur'ān, though before it thou was one of the heedless. (Yusuf 12:3)

The distinction of Qur'ānic stories over others include:

1. Stories narrated by Allah – "We will relate"
2. They have a goal –

نَّقُصُّ عَلَيْكَ مِنْ أَنبَاءِ الرُّسُلِ مَا نُثَبِّتُ بِهِ فُؤَادَكَ

We relate to thee of the tidings of the Messengers is that whereby We strengthen thy heart. (Hūd 11:120).

3. They are fact, not fiction –

نَقُصُّ عَلَيْكَ نَبَأَهُم بِالْحَقِّ

relate to thee their tidings truly (Al Kahf 18:13).

4. Based on science, not conjecture –

فَلَنَقُصَّنَّ عَلَيْهِم بِعِلْمٍ

We shall relate to them with knowledge (Al Arāf 7:7).

5. A tool of contemplation, not stupefaction –

فَاقْصُصِ الْقَصَصَ لَعَلَّهُمْ يَتَفَكَّرُونَ

So relate the story; haply they will reflect (Al Arāf 7:176).

6. A tool of education, not entertainment.

لَقَدْ كَانَ فِي قَصَصِهِمْ عِبْرَةٌ

In their stories is surely a lesson (Yusuf 12:111).

Variety of Reciters of The Holy Qur'ān

{وَإِذَا قُرِئَ الْقُرْآنُ فَاسْتَمِعُوا لَهُ وَأَنصِتُوا لَعَلَّكُمْ تُرْحَمُونَ}

And when the Holy Qur'ān is recited, give you ear to it and be silent; haply so you will find mercy. (Al Arāf 7:204)

Imam Bāqir states that there are three groups of reciters of the Qur'ān:

• A group that considers the Holy Qur'ān a form of earning income and work and to pay for their living expenses, impose upon others this expectation.

- A group that only bring to life the Holy Qur'ān through their tongue but with regards to practical application, do not care for its laws.
- And a group that have recited the Holy Qur'ān and know it as medicine for their pain and are intimate with the Qur'ān, and Allahﷻ will with this medium protect these individuals from torment and for their sake will cause rain to fall, and such people are very rare.[1]

---

[1] (Al Kafi) V2 P627

Lesson 5 Supplication

The Importance of Supplication

$$\{قُلْ مَا يَعْبَؤُاْ بِكُمْ رَبِّي لَوْ لَا دُعَاؤُكُمْ فَقَدْ كَذَّبْتُمْ فَسَوْفَ يَكُونُ لِزَامًا\}$$

Say: 'My Lord esteems you not at all were it not for your supplication, for you have cried lies, and it shall surely be fastened. (Al Furqān 25:77)

The sentence "My Lord esteems you not at all were it not for your supplication" indicates that the Lord does not hold for a group of people any value, due to their past actions, had they not been under the shadow of their supplications and worship.

Of course, with regards to the words "your supplication", there are two meanings. One is supplication and crying with special attention to Allah, such is in the narrations when we read: A person of supplication is a person who will not perish.[1] So from a group of people who were not of those who supplicated, the complaint will be that instead of supplication, you opted to go towards idols, desires and tyrants, and so retribution will be seen. And one where the meaning is the invitation from Allah to people, because His Divine Tradition is one that invites people with Truth and complete proof

---

[1] (Al Kafi) V4 P228

over them. What makes one a better presence and of more value is the very acceptance of the invitation of Allah✳, yet you did not accept the invitation and belied it, so hope of good in you is non-existent and retribution for your action will be delivered.

In one place Allah✳ states in the Holy Qur'ān

{وَمَا خَلَقْتُ الْجِنَّ وَالْإِنسَ إِلَّا لِيَعْبُدُونِ}

I have not created jinn and mankind except to serve Me. (Ad Dhariyāt 51:56)

And when combined with the Ayah above, that had it not been for your supplication you would not have had any value, it is apparent the supplication is the heart and soul of worship.

Yes, even with the fact the Allah✳ is All Knowing of everything, yet supplication remains our duty. Supplication in every place and at every moment is beneficial. This is because Allah✳ states:

{فَإِنِّي قَرِيبٌ}

I am near (Al Baqarah 2:186)

So, if we are sometimes recipients of the wrath of Allah✳, it is because the distance we have placed between ourselves and Allah✳ through the effect of sin.

The Attention of Allah✳ to those who Supplicate

{وَإِذَا سَأَلَكَ عِبَادِى عَنِّي فَإِنِّي قَرِيبٌ أُجِيبُ دَعْوَةَ الدَّاعِ إِذَا دَعَانِ فَلْيَسْتَجِيبُواْ لِي وَ لْيُؤْمِنُواْ بِي لَعَلَّهُمْ يَرْشُدُونَ}

And when __My__ servants question thee concerning __Me__ -- __I__ am near to (I) answer the call of the caller, when he calls to __Me__; so let them respond to __Me__, and let them believe in __Me__; haply so they will go aright. (Al Baqarah 2:186).

Supplication is a reason for so much affection from the Lord that in this Ayah, Allah✳ uses the first-person pronoun seven times (see underlined words above). This affection occurs in the instance where the person wants to seek help from Allah✳ through supplication.

Question: Why is it that sometimes our supplications are not answered?

Answer: In "Al-Mizan: An Exegesis of the Qur'ān", we read that in this Ayah, Allah◉ states that

{أُجِيبُ دَعْوَةَ الدَّاعِ إِذَا دَعَانِ}

I answer the call of the caller, when he calls to Me

(Al Baqarah 2:186).

Allah◉ will answer the call of the caller that only calls upon Him, with complete sincerity, and requests good. So, if a supplication has not been answered, it is either because our request from Allah◉ was not for the better, and in reality would have been for the worse for us, or if it was in reality for the better for us, we did not request frankly and with complete sincerity where it was contaminated with an appeal to others. Or it could be that the answering of the supplication would not lead to our benefit, such as that stated in the narrations, in such cases we are protected from calamity, or our future generations are protected or compensation is granted in the Hereafter.

In Usul Kafi, we read that the one who consumes what is unlawful or does not enjoin good and forbid evil, and who supplicates without attention or presence of the heart, their supplications are not answered.

The meaning of supplication is not to leave earning a living and work, but rather reliance upon Allah◉ along with effort. That's why in the narrations we read: Supplication without effort will not be answered.

Perhaps the placement of an Ayah of supplication in amongst Ayāt relating to fasting is due to it being more appropriate that the month of Allah◉ be spent along with supplication.

Question: Given that the work of Allah◉ is fixed based upon law and based upon deeds and traditions, what role does supplication play?

Answer: Just as the rules relating to the prayers and fasts of a traveller are different to that of one who is in their own residence, one who supplicates is different to one who is negligent of Allah◉ and the tradition of Allah◉ benefits the former, not the latter. Yes, supplications and conversations with Allah◉ increase the capacity of one to be able to accept the beneficence of Allah◉. Likewise, the invocation and the visitation of vicegerents (اوليا) of

Allah✺ changes the condition that one is in. Just like if a father takes along his child as a guest, the host will accept them with more love and affection than if they went alone. So, supplication, visitation and invocation is the reason for the changing of conditions of someone, not the disruption of the Absolute Divine tradition.

The Etiquette of Supplication

{وَ قَالَ رَبُّكُمُ ادْعُونِي أَسْتَجِبْ لَكُمْ إِنَّ الَّذِينَ يَسْتَكْبِرُونَ عَنْ عِبَادَتِي سَيَدْخُلُونَ جَهَنَّمَ دَاخِرِينَ}

And your Lord hath said: Pray unto Me and I will hear your prayer. Lo! those
who scorn My service, they will enter hell, disgrace (Ghāfir 40:60).

Supplications have etiquettes and conditions that need to be met including:

I.   Supplication must be with faith and deed.

{يَسْتَجِيبُ الَّذِينَ آمَنُوا وَعَمِلُوا الصَّالِحَاتِ }

He answers those who believe and do righteous deeds (Al Shurā 42:26).

II.   With sincerity

{فَادْعُوا اللَّـهَ مُخْلِصِينَ}

So call unto God sincerely (Ghāfir 40:14).

III.   With humbleness and in secret

{ادْعُوا رَبَّكُمْ تَضَرُّعًا وَخُفْيَةً}

Call on your Lord, humbly and secretly (Al A'rāf 7:55).

IV.   With fear and hope

{وَادْعُوهُ خَوْفًا وَطَمَعًا}

And call unto Him with in fear and hope. (Al A'rāf 7:56).

V.   During some special hours

{يَدْعُونَ رَبَّهُم بِالْغَدَاةِ وَالْعَشِيِّ }

Call upon their Lord at morning and evening (Al Anām 6:52).

VI. The one who is supplicating should benefit from the heavenly divine names.

{وَلِلَّـهِ الْأَسْمَاءُ الْحُسْنَىٰ فَادْعُوهُ بِهَا}

To God belong the Names Most Beautiful; so call Him by them (Al A'rāf 7:180).

Of course, we must bring to attention that some deeds such as sin, oppression, and not forgiving those who have sought forgiveness from us, are a barrier to the answering of supplication. Or sometimes, the answering of a supplication means the need to break the world order of creation. Like the example of the student that answered a geography question incorrectly, that the surface of the sea is higher than that of the mountain top, the student requested from Allah that the two be swapped. Anyway, Allah being All Able, is also All Wise.

The answering of supplication is two sided. That means that if people are awaiting the answering of their supplication, they also need to answer and accept the invitation of Allah so that your supplication can also be answered by Allah.

{اسْتَجِيبُوا لِلَّـهِ وَلِلرَّسُولِ إِذَا دَعَاكُمْ لِمَا يُحْيِيكُمْ}

respond to God and the Messenger when He calls you unto that which will give you life (Al Anfāl 8:24).

The Beautiful Names of Allah

{وَلِلَّـهِ الْأَسْمَاءُ الْحُسْنَىٰ فَادْعُوهُ بِهَا}

To God belong the Names Most Beautiful; so call Him by them (Al A'rāf 7:180).

Although all Divine names and attributes are beautiful and good, and Allah has all the Perfection which cannot be comprehended nor counted, in the narrations we have 99 names which have been emphasised and anyone who calls upon Allah with these names will have their supplications answered.

In the Qur'ān, up to 145 names of Allah are noted and 99 names in the narrations, either because some of the names can be combined and are practically applied to be the same as each other, or it could mean that the names of Allah are not limited to a number. In some narrations and supplications there are even more names that have been noted, like in the supplication of Jawshan Kabīr. Of course, some of the Divine Beautiful Names have special effects, blessings and importance.

Imam Riḍa⁣ states: We, the Purified Household, are the Beautiful Names of Allah for which the deed of none will be accepted without comprehending us.

نحن والله الأسماء الحسنى التي لا يقبل الله من العباد عملا إلا بمعرفتنا[1]

He also stated any time you come across problems and hardship, invoke help from Allah though us as a medium, and then recited.

﴿وَلِلَّـهِ الْأَسْمَاءُ الْحُسْنَىٰ فَادْعُوهُ بِهَا﴾

To God belong the Names Most Beautiful; so call Him by them. (Al A'rāf 7:180).

It has also been narrated from him that he stated:

إن الخالق لا يوصف إلا بما وصف به نفسه

The Creator cannot be described except with how He described Himself.

That means we cannot ascribe names to Allah of our own, such as calling him chaste, brave and the like. [2]

---

[1] (تفسير اثنا عشرى - Twelver Interpretation)
[2] (تفسير فرقان - Tafseer Furqan)

Lesson 6 Importance of Prayers

Luqmān's Advice

{يَابُنَيَّ أَقِمِ الصَّلَوةَ وَ أْمُرْ بِالْمَعْرُوفِ وَ انْهَ عَنِ الْمُنكَرِ
وَ اصْبِرْ عَلَى مَا أَصَابَكَ إِنَّ ذَالِكَ مِنْ عَزْمِ الْأُمُورِ}

O my son, perform the prayer, and Enjoin Good and Forbid Evil. And bear
patiently whatever may befall you; surely that (patience) is true constancy (Of
importance and what is obligatory). (Luqmān 31:17).

A summary with regards to the advice that Prophet Luqmān﷿ gave to his son concerning prayers and enjoining is as follows:

- Prayers is the simplest, deepest, and most beautiful method of communication and connection with Allahﷻ which was part and parcel of all heavenly religions.
- Prayers is the only worship for which it has been advised to, before performing it, to have those with the best voices to rise and with a loud voice, invite to prayer through the slogans "Hasten to prayer, Hasten to success, Hasten to the best deed". With it, silence is broken and another cycle of the pure thoughts if Islam is declared and those who are neglectful are awakened.

- Prayers is so important that aim of settling Prophet Abrahams⍨ wife and son in the dry, arid and waterless lands of Mecca was to uphold the prayer, not the pilgrimage rites.

- Imam Husain⍨, for the sake of performing prayers during midday on the Day of Ashura, was struck in the shield of his chest by the arrows of the enemy.

- The Holy Qur'ān conveys the order to Prophets Abraham ⍨ and Ismael ⍨ to build and purify the Masjid Al Harām (The Mosque in Mecca) in preparation for those who perform prayers. Yes, prayers are so important that Zakaria, Maryam, Abraham, Ismael where all servants of places of worship and where prayers were performed.

- Prayer of an individual is in effect from the time of birth, in which a newborn has the Adhan and Iqama recited in their ears, through to after death, where the prayer of the deceased is performed upon the body in the cemetery.

- Prayer is the key to the acceptance to all deeds and Imam Ali⍨ advices his governor to ensure his best time is reserved for prayers and to be aware that all of their actions will be accepted in light of their prayers.

- Prayer is the remembrance of Allah⍨. And remembrance of Allah⍨ is the only calmer of the heart.

- Prayer is proposed in most Surah's of the Holy Qur'ān form the longest Surah (Al Baqarah) though to the shortest (Kawthar).

- There are prayers for earthly events such as earthquakes and strong winds that instil fear, as well as heavenly events such as eclipses where prayers become obligatory. There are even prayers prescribed for requesting rain.

- Prayers keeps one from committing many vices and obscenities.

In prayers, our attention and desires are directed towards perfection, consider the following:

- Cleanliness and hygiene, in everything such as brushing teeth, ablution, ghusl[1], cleanliness of the body and cloths.
- Valour, audacity and calling loudly is learnt from the Call to Prayer.

---

[1] A methodological and systematic approach, with intention, to cleansing the body necessary after certain events such as a women cycle, intercourse, or touching the deceased.

- Presence in an arena is taught through Mosques.
- Attention to justice is considered through the selection of a just person to be leader of the congregation.
- Attention is drawn to the perfection and value of those who stand in the first line of the congregational prayer.
- Independent orientation is felt through the Qibla. Jews perform their worship in one direction and Christians in another, while Muslims must also have their own independent direction to face, therefore as the Holy Qur'ān states, The Ka'ba is the independent Qibla of Muslims so that they find their independence.
- Attention to the rights of others – by way of prayers having to be performed with clothing worn that has not been usurped, not even a single thread of it.
- Attention towards political movements is felt here where we read in the narrations: Prayers are not accepted where they are not combined with the acceptance of the Guardian and Divinely Guided Leader.
- Attention is brought to order through straight lines in which we pray congregational prayers in, and attention towards martyrs using the soil of Karbala to prostrate on, and attention to surrounding hygiene and cleanliness which are as per recommendations given for the cleanliness and purity of Mosques and Mosque goers.
- Attention is brought towards Allahﷻ during the entire prayer, attention to resurrection while reciting "Master of the Day of Judgment" (Al Fātiha 1:4), attention to the path we choose to take through "Show us the straightway" (Al Fātiha 1:6), attention to choosing the right people to associate with through "the path of those whom Thou hast blessed" (Al Fātiha 1:7), and avoiding association with those who have strayed and who have wrath upon them through "not of those against whom Thou art wrathful, nor of those who are astray" (Al Fātiha 1:7), attention towards the Prophetﷺ and his pure progeny through the Tashahhud and towards the pure and righteous ones through the greetings "Peace be upon us and upon Allah'sﷻ righteous worshippers."
- We see attention to healthy nutrition here through advice such as anyone who consumes alcoholic drinks, will not have their prayers accepted for 40 days.

– Apparent adornments are seen here through advice that the best clothes, perfume and ornaments should be utilised in prayer and even women are advised to wear adornments during prayers.
– Attention is brought towards our spouses where we read in the narrations that should we have quarrelled with or annoyed our spouse or spoken badly to them, the prayers of neither of them will be accepted.

In the Ayāt of the Qur'ān, "prayers" and the "Enjoining good and forbidding evil" appear together and affect each other, such as in the following Ayāt:

{إِنَّ الصَّلَاةَ تَنْهَىٰ عَنِ الْفَحْشَاءِ وَالْمُنكَرِ}

Lo! worship preserves from lewdness and iniquity (Al Ankabūt 29:45).

{إِنَّ الْحَسَنَاتِ يُذْهِبْنَ السَّيِّئَاتِ}

Lo! good deeds (such as prayers) annul ill-deeds (Hud 11:114).

{أَقِمِ الصَّلَاةَ وَأْمُرْ بِالْمَعْرُوفِ وَانْهَ عَنِ الْمُنكَرِ}

Perform the prayer, and enjoin the good and forbid the evil (Luqmān 31:17).

{الَّذِينَ إِن مَّكَّنَّاهُمْ فِي الْأَرْضِ أَقَامُوا الصَّلَاةَ وَآتَوُا الزَّكَاةَ وَأَمَرُوا بِالْمَعْرُوفِ وَنَهَوْا عَنِ الْمُنكَرِ}

Those who, if We give them power in the land, establish worship and pay the poor-due and enjoin good and forbid evil (Al Hajj 22:41).

Lesson 7 Enjoining Good and Forbidding Evil

Importance of Enjoining Good and Forbidding Evil

{وَلْتَكُن مِّنكُمْ أُمَّةٌ يَدْعُونَ إِلَى ٱلْخَيْرِ وَيَأْمُرُونَ بِالْمَعْرُوفِ
وَيَنْهَوْنَ عَنِ ٱلْمُنكَرِ وَأُولَٰئِكَ هُمُ ٱلْمُفْلِحُونَ}

And there may spring from you a nation who invite to goodness, and enjoin right conduct and forbid indecency. Such are they who are successful. (Āle Imrān 3:104).

Enjoining right conduct means advice to do good and forbid indecency and to arrest or detain the doing of evil. The accomplishment of these two orders is not limited to a specific age group, and thus Luqmān(a) says to his son"

{يَا بُنَيَّ أَقِمِ الصَّلَاةَ وَأْمُرْ بِالْمَعْرُوفِ وَانْهَ عَنِ الْمُنكَرِ}

O my dear son! Establish worship and enjoin kindness and forbid iniquity... (Luqmān 31:17).

Enjoining good is a sign of love for faith, love for the people, a desire for the wellbeing of society and a sign of freedom of expression, religious zeal, a friendly association with other people, a sign of an awakened natural instinct, general control and presence in the society.

Enjoining the good and forbidding the evil is the reason for encouragement of those who do good, making aware those who were ignorant, being aware for the prevention of offenses and the formation of a form of societal control. The Holy Qur'ān states:

{كُنتُمْ خَيْرَ أُمَّةٍ أُخْرِجَتْ لِلنَّاسِ تَأْمُرُونَ بِالْمَعْرُوفِ وَتَنْهَوْنَ عَنِ الْمُنكَرِ}

You are the best nation ever brought forth to men, bidding to honour, and

forbidding dishonour (Āle Imrān 3:110).

Imam Ali[ﷺ] states that enjoining the good and forbidding the evil is in the interest of the public.[1] Likewise in another narration, we read anyone who does not stand against evil is like someone who leaves an injured on the road until they pass away.[2]

Prophets like David and Jesus peace upon them would curse upon those who do not stand against evil.

{لُعِنَ الَّذِينَ كَفَرُوا مِن بَنِي إِسْرَائِيلَ عَلَىٰ لِسَانِ دَاوُودَ وَعِيسَى ابْنِ مَرْيَمَ}

Cursed were the unbelievers of the Children of Israel by the tongue of David, and

Jesus, Mary's son (Māida 5:78).

The revolution of Imam Husain[ﷺ] was for the enjoining the good and forbidding the evil, "I want to enjoin good and forbid evil".[3]

Silence and indifference in the face of sin is the reason for the normalisation of sinning, those who sin find courage, we become heavy hearted, Satan finds contentment and Allah[ﷻ] will be displeased with us.

The Holy Qur'ān states that if you find yourself in the company of those who insult the Holy Qur'ān, leave the company in protest until such time the conversation changes.

If one invites another to do good deed, a partnership in the reward is forged, but if in the face of corruption, deviation and sin we sit silently, step by step the corruption grows, and corrupt and seditious individuals will end up

---

[1] (Nahjul Balagha) Hikmah 252

[2] (Kanz Ul Amal – كنز العمال) V3, P170

[3] (Bihar Al Anwar بحار الأنوار) V44 p328

governing society. One must at the onset of sin, not only show displeasure with the tongue and forbidding the evil, but also utilise all available legal avenues and abilities to end the continuation of evil.

Enjoining the good and forbidding the evil are two divinely ordained laws, and the imagination that, *"the sin that others do have nothing to do with me, and we should not take away the freedom of others, I am a shy and scared person, one change won't make any difference anyway, Jesus has his religion and Moses has his religion, we won't be buried in the same grave, there are others, why should I be the one forbidding evil?, by forbidding evil, friends and customers will walk away"*, and other examples like these, are not able to lift this responsibility from our shoulders.

Manners And Conditions

Enjoining the good and forbidding the evil must be done with knowledge, a soft heart, with wisdom, and even with a level of secrecy. Sometimes it is us that must do the talking, but where we won't make any impression, the duty does not lapse, but rather we must seek the assistance of others so that they may speak up. Even if we can just for a small period forbid corruption, we must forbid it and if repetition can lead to a result, we must repeat.

Enjoining the good and forbidding the evil can be conducted in two ways:

1. Through general responsibility of everyone where all participate to the extent of their own abilities.
2. A responsibility of a group of organisations that are held responsible for and of the following up of such matters and are able to act upon such issues with power.

Such as the example of a driver that drives in the wrong direction, both the drivers of other vehicles object to the offending driver with their car horns and beam lights and also the police can issue punishments in line with the offence such infringement notices, impound the vehicle or withdraw the drivers licence of the offender.

Enjoining The Good, Is A Sign of The Best Nation

{كُنتُمْ خَيْرَ أُمَّةٍ أُخْرِجَتْ لِلنَّاسِ تَأْمُرُونَ بِالْمَعْرُوفِ وَتَنْهَوْنَ عَنِ الْمُنكَرِ وَتُؤْمِنُونَ بِاللَّـهِ}

You are the best nation ever brought forth to men, bidding to honour, and forbidding dishonour, and believing in God. ... (Āle Imrān 3:110).

This ayah points to the general requirement to enjoin good and forbid evil with conditions and points to consider including:

1. Being the best nation is not a slogan, enjoining good and forbidding evil with faith and belief: "You are the best nation… promoting good".
2. A nation of silent and fearful people is not the best of nations: "You are the best nation… promoting good… forbidding evil".
3. Enjoining good and forbidding evil is of such importance it is a measure of distinction of the nation: "You are the best nation".
4. Enjoining good and forbidding evil is achieved once Muslims act as one nation, i.e. a sovereign nation: "You are the best nation".
5. Muslims are responsible for the reformation of all other communities: "brought forth to men".
6. Advice to do good without the struggle to end evil comes to little fruition: "bidding to honour and forbidding dishonour".
7. Every member of the nation must contribute to enjoining good and forbidding evil (A nine-year-old girl has that entitlement over the president of the nation).
8. On the issue of enjoining good, age, location, race, literacy, economic or social status has no relevance: "You are the best nation… bidding…. forbidding".
9. Muslims must be positioned to enjoin good and forbid evil with authority, not with weakness and entreaty: "Bidding".
10. Enjoining good precedes forbidding evil: "Bidding… forbidding".
11. Enjoining good and forbidding evil can be effective when its foundation is rooted in faith: "Bidding, forbidding… believing".

Effects And Blessings

A hint at the effects and blessings of enjoining good and forbidding evil, even in the instance where it has no effect (on others), is indicated below:

1. Sometimes, the effect is not apparent immediately, but in history we see the nature and judgement of others have an effect. Such as the martyrdom of Imam Husain in his mission to enjoin good and forbid evil, which has awakened the conscience of mankind throughout history.
2. Sometimes the bidding and forbidding is to protect the space for others. The call to prayers, the Adhan, is recommended even if there

is no one to hear it. Stopping at a red traffic light is an obligation, even if there are no other cars. Therefore, the preservation of the law, space and the respect of the law, is an obligation.

3. Sometimes the sinner may not stop committing their sin, but successive reminders will leave a bitter taste in their mouth and at least would not be committing the sin with ease of mind, and one day, their conscience will awaken and be affected.

4. For the protection of freedom, it is necessary to enjoin good and forbid evil, for otherwise society will be turned into an environment of palpitation, fear, and silence.

5. Enjoining good and forbidding evil is for mankind a praiseworthy task, even if others do not listen. The Holy Qur'ān states.

$$\{وَمَنْ أَحْسَنُ قَوْلًا مِّمَّن دَعَا إِلَى اللَّـهِ\}$$

And who is better in speech than he who invites to Allah (Fussilat 41:33).

6. If we are not able to affect the actions of others, at least for our own sake it is a one form of nearness to Allahﷻ, inculcation, practicing bravery, facing pain and engagement.

7. Enjoining good will provide salvation from the wrath of Allahﷻ.

8. Enjoining and forbidding gives some form of contentment to consciousness, one would say to themselves that I have fulfilled my duty. This contentment is valuable, even if others do not listen.

Enjoining good and forbidding evil is the way of the Prophets, even if others did not listen. The Holy Qur'ān states multiple times that people did not heed the warnings and right path of the Prophets and turned their backs against them. They fulfilled their religious duties and were martyred in the path of enjoining good and forbidding evil so that the Truth is not lost.

Lesson 8 Commentary on Surah Hamd

بِسْمِ اللَّـهِ الرَّحْمَـٰنِ الرَّحِيمِ ﴿١﴾

الْحَمْدُ لِلَّـهِ رَبِّ الْعَالَمِينَ ﴿٢﴾الرَّحْمَـٰنِ الرَّحِيمِ ﴿٣﴾

مَالِكِ يَوْمِ الدِّينِ ﴿٤﴾ إِيَّاكَ نَعْبُدُ وَإِيَّاكَ نَسْتَعِينُ ﴿٥﴾ اهْدِنَا الصِّرَاطَ الْمُسْتَقِيمَ ﴿٦﴾ صِرَاطَ الَّذِينَ أَنْعَمْتَ عَلَيْهِمْ غَيْرِ الْمَغْضُوبِ عَلَيْهِمْ وَلَا الضَّالِّينَ ﴿٧﴾

In the Name of Allah, the Merciful, the Compassionate; Praise belongs to God, the Lord of all Being; the All-merciful, the All-compassionate; the Master of the Day of Judgment; Thee only we serve; to Thee alone we pray for succour; Guide us in the straight path; the path of those whom Thou hast blessed, not of those against whom Thou art wrathful, nor of those who are astray. (Al Hamd 1:1-7).

{الْحَمْدُ لِلَّـهِ}Is the best form in which to thank Allah۞ with. Anyone, anywhere, with any language, any form of praise of any perfection or beauty, is praising the source of the perfection and beauty. Of course, praising Allah۞ is not inconsistent with praising the created on the condition that it be in the matter of Allah۞ and in His line and path.

Allah۞ has made it incumbent upon Himself to be merciful:

{كَتَبَ رَبُّكُمْ عَلَىٰ نَفْسِهِ الرَّحْمَةَ}

Your Lord hath inscribed for Himself (the rule of) mercy.

(Al-Inām 6:54).

And the shadow of His mercy is spread over all things.

$$\{وَرَحْمَتِي وَسِعَتْ كُلَّ شَىْءٍ\}$$

My mercy extends to all things. (Al A'rāf 7:156)

Likewise, the Prophetﷺ and his book is the source of Mercy

$$\{رَحْمَةً لِّلْعَالَمِينَ\}$$

A Mercy to the worlds (Al Ambiyā 21:107).

His creation and nourishment are based upon mercy and if punishment is given it too, is from the point of view of kindness.

The pardoning of sins, acceptance of repentance and the concealment of their shortfalls and the giving of an opportunity to make up for mistakes, are all manifestations of His mercy and kindness.

Notwithstanding that Allahﷻ is always the True owner of all things, his ownership on the day of judgement and resurrection is of a different manifestation.

The sentence "we serve" also points to this in that prayers prayed in congregation shows that all Muslims are brothers and on the one path, in prayers, even though one person is representing all the worshippers in saying Oh Lord, not only am I but all of us are your worshippers, and not only I but all of us are in need of your kindness.

This surah introduces the straight path as the path of those who have been blessed with the Divine favours and consist of: The Prophets, the truthful ones, martyrs and pious ones[1]. Directing our attention to the path of those magnanimous people and our hopes being in them and inculcating this hope in ourselves, we are taken back from the deviated and dangerous paths. And after desire, we seek from Allahﷻ that He does not allow us to follow the path of those whose Gods wrath is upon or have gone astray.

---

[1] وَمَن يُطِعِ اللَّـهَ وَالرَّسُولَ فَأُولَٰئِكَ مَعَ الَّذِينَ أَنْعَمَ اللَّـهُ عَلَيْهِم مِّنَ النَّبِيِّينَ وَالصِّدِّيقِينَ وَالشُّهَدَاءِ وَحَسُنَ أُولَٰئِكَ رَفِيقًا وَالصَّالِحِينَ

(And whoever obeys Allah and the Apostle, these are with those upon whom Allah has bestowed favours from among the prophets and the truthful and the martyrs and the good, and a goodly company are they!) An Nisā 4:69.

The meaning of "Thou has blessed" is the blessing of Guidance. Such is why the Ayah before was with respect to guidance. As well as that there are the material blessings of the disbelievers and astray and others.

Even if we are guided, it is still a dangerous course to traverse, and we must always seek from Allah﷾ the path that is not the paths of those whom Gods wrath is upon or have gone astray.

Educational Lessons from Surah Hamd

1. With بِسْمِ اللَّـهِ we cut all hope from all other than Allah﷾.
2. With مَالِكِ يَوْمِ الدِّينِ and رَبِّ الْعَالَمِينَ we feel that all ownership and nourishment belongs to Allah﷾ and on that basis we should place aside all selfishness and vanity.
3. With the word الْعَالَمِينَ we see ourselves as a part of disciplined existence and far from being a solo and isolated life.
4. With الرَّحْمَـٰنِ الرَّحِيمِ we see ourselves under the shadow of His kindness.
5. With مَالِكِ يَوْمِ الدِّينِ neglect from the future is filed away.
6. By saying إِيَّاكَ نَعْبُدُ hypocrisy and the desire for fame is disappears.
7. With وَإِيَّاكَ نَسْتَعِينُ with nothing but the power of Allah﷾ do we seek shelter.
8. With saying أَنْعَمْتَ we acknowledge that from Him are all blessings.
9. With اهْدِنَا guidance is sought to The True and Correct Path and The Straight Path.
10. With صِرَاطَ الَّذِينَ أَنْعَمْتَ عَلَيْهِمْ we announce our association with the followers of Truth.
11. With saying غَيْرِ الْمَغْضُوبِ عَلَيْهِمْ وَلَا الضَّالِّينَ disgust at and distancing oneself is expressed. A distancing from falsehood and those who follow it.

The Importance Of بِسْمِ اللَّـهِ

{بِسْمِ اللَّـهِ الرَّحْمَـٰنِ الرَّحِيمِ}

In the name of Allah, the Beneficent, the Merciful.

بِسْمِ اللَّـهِ الرَّحْمَـٰنِ الرَّحِيمِ Is not only the beginning of the Qur'ān, but is the start of all the Heavenly Books. The start of all of the tasks and works of the all the Prophets began with "In the Name of Allah﷾". Prophet Sulaimān﷿ also started his letter to Queen Sheba with the sentence بِسْمِ اللَّـهِ الرَّحْمَـٰنِ الرَّحِيمِ.

Imam Ali stated that the words بِسْمِ اللَّـهِ is the source of blessing of our work and its omission is the cause of a bad ending. The utterance of the words بِسْمِ اللَّـهِ is recommended to begin any work, when eating and sleeping and sitting, riding, travelling and many other tasks, even where an animal is slaughtered without the name of Allah, its meat become sinful to consume.

بِسْمِ اللَّـهِ is the slogan and token of Muslims and all works performed by Muslims must have a tinge of Divinity in it. Just like how the products of a manufacturer have the logo and symbols of that manufacturer imprinted on their products, whether partially or in its entirety. Or like the flag representing the country being perched on the desks and offices of administrative buildings, schools, garrisons, national ships of that country sailing the high seas.

Imam Sādiq has been narrated to have stated that بِسْمِ اللَّـهِ is the crown of the Surahs. The only surah in the Holy Qur'ān which does not start with this Ayah is Surah of Bara'āt[1] (or repentance, ninth surah), and according to Imam Ali, this is because بِسْمِ اللَّـهِ are the words of security and mercy while the proclamation of this Surah is the disownment from disbelievers and polytheists and is not compatible to start with the words showing affection[2].

بِسْمِ اللَّـهِ causes the Satan to flee. Anyone who is accompanied by Allah, Satan will not be able to influence.

The Straight Path

صِّرَاط is the name of a bridge crossing over Hell which on the day of resurrection all people must cross over.

In the quest for being on the Straight (Path), the one and only request that every Muslim requests from Allah in every prayer, even the Prophet and his Purified Household, peace and blessings be upon them, request that they remain on the Straight Path.

The Straight Path has levels and stages:

$$\{وَالَّذِينَ اهْتَدَوْا زَادَهُمْ هُدًى\}$$

those who are guided aright, them He increases in guidance (Muḥammad 47:17).

---

[1] To declare innocence from any association with another – disownment.
[2] Tafsir Qartabi and Majma Albayān

Even those who are on the True Path such as the Saints of Allah﷾ (Divinely Guided), must supplicate in order to remain on that path and to further illuminate their guidance.

The Straight Path means moderation and temperance, and abstinence from any form of excessiveness and delinquency, whether it be in faith or in action.

In narrations, the Divinely Guided^ state that, "We are the Straight Path"[1]. Meaning they are the Divine Guides, perfect theoretical and practical examples of the Straight Path and role models in following their footsteps in that path. They provide guidance in all aspects of our life from work, pleasure, earning, feeding, spending, criticising, anger, compromise, relations with children etc., and advise us to live in moderation and temperance.[2] Interestingly, it is on this very same Straight Path that Satan lies in ambush:

{لَأَقْعُدَنَّ لَهُمْ صِرَاطَكَ الْمُسْتَقِيمَ}

I (Satan) shall surely sit in ambush for them on Thy straight path (Al A'rāf 7:16).

In the Holy Qur'ān and narrations many examples are present with regards to emphasising temperance on the Straight Path and abstinence from excessiveness and delinquency. Islam does not look at only one dimension that looks at only one aspect and ignores all others; but rather in every part action temperance and moderation and the straight path is recommended.

Wrath in The Holy Qur'ān

In the Qur'ān, people such as Pharaoh, Qarun, Abu Lahab and such nations as Aad, Bani Israel, are identified as those who have Wrath upon them and some have been named as those who have strayed such as Satan, Pharaoh, Samirī, bad friends, deviated leaders and ancestors. In numerous Ayāt, the characteristics of those who have strayed and who have attracted wrath upon themselves and their instances have been presented.

We, in every prayer, request that we don't end up being like those have had wrath upon them. That means we desire not to be from the people who deviate and consume usury, nor of those who escape struggles. Likewise, we desire not to be of those who have gone astray, those who have parted from the Path of Truth and who chase the falsehood and in religion and our own

---

[1] (Bihar Al Anwar بحار الأنوار) V87 P3
[2] (Al Kafi) – Chapter of Economy and Worship

beliefs, exaggerate and are extravagant, or who follow their own whims and desires or those of others.

The foundations for deviation in according to the Holy Qur'ān develops from

1. Fantasies and vain desires[1]: اتَّخَذَ إِلَـهَهُ هَوَاهُ وَأَضَلَّهُ اللَّـهُ
2. Idols[2]: وَجَعَلُوا لِلَّـهِ أَندَادًا لِّيُضِلُّوا عَن سَبِيلِهِ
3. Sins[3]: وَمَا يُضِلُّ بِهِ إِلَّا الْفَاسِقِينَ
4. The acceptance of false guardianship [4]: أَنَّهُ مَن تَوَلَّاهُ فَأَنَّهُ يُضِلُّهُ
5. Ignorance and foolishness[5]: وَإِن كُنتُم مِّن قَبْلِهِ لَمِنَ الضَّالِّينَ

Mankind in this Surah testifies and expresses the passion, interest and self-navigation towards Prophets and martyrs and the pious and their path, and declares innocence and distance from the recipients of wrath and those who have strayed in history. That is the application of association and disownment.[6]

---

[1] him who has taken his caprice to be his god, and God has led him astray (Al Jāthiya 45:23)

[2] And they set up compeers to God, that they might lead astray from His way. (Ibrahīm 14:30)

[3] He leads none astray save the ungodly (Baqarah 2:26)

[4] that whosoever takes him for a friend, him he leads astray (Al Hajj 22:4)

[5] though formerly you were gone astray. (Baqarah 2:198)

[6] تولی و تبری

Lesson 9 Night Prayers

{وَمِنَ اللَّيْلِ فَتَهَجَّدْ بِهِ نَافِلَةً لَّكَ عَسَىٰ

أَن يَبْعَثَكَ رَبُّكَ مَقَامًا مَّحْمُودًا}

And as for the night, keep vigil a part of it, as a work of supererogation for thee; it may be that thy Lord will raise thee up to a laudable station. (Isrā 17:79).

"هجود" gives the meaning of sleep and "تهجد" gives the meaning of keeping away from sleep with acts of worship. In the word مَقَامًا there is a hidden meaning (due to the ◌ٌ vowel) and in narrations, مَقَامًا مَّحْمُودًا (*laudable station*) is that very intercession.

Three things were obligatory upon the Prophetﷺ and that are recommended to all of us: Night prayers, use of miswak[1], and rising early in the morning.

Night prayers is a prayer full of virtue and in Surahs Muzammil and Mudathir the recommendation was emphasised:

{قُمِ اللَّيْلَ إِلَّا قَلِيلًا}

Keep vigil the night, except a little (Al Muzzammil 73:2).

---

[1] Tooth cleansing twig.

In narrations, more than 30 virtues have been listed for night prayers, some of which are listed below:

- All of the Prophets performed night prayers. Night prayers is the secret of a healthy body and the light of the grave. The night prayers will positively affect one's manners and etiquettes, daily earnings and wealth, keeps away sorrow and grief, tools of religion, the enlightenment of the face and the brightening of the eyes.
- Night prayers suppresses the sins of the day and is the light of the Day of Judgement.
- Imam Sādiq⁽ᵃ⁾ states the reward of Night Prayers is so much so that Allah says

$$\{فَلَا تَعْلَمُ نَفْسٌ مَّا أُخْفِيَ لَهُم مِّن قُرَّةِ أَعْيُنٍ$$
$$جَزَاءً بِمَا كَانُوا يَعْمَلُونَ\}$$

No soul knows what comfort is laid up for them secretly, as a recompense for that they were doing. (Sajda 32:17).

- Imam Sādiq⁽ᵃ⁾ states the honour of a believer is the Night Prayer and his glory is not hurting and persecuting people.
- We read in the narration that unfortunate is the one that is deprived of Night Prayers.
- Abu Dhar, next to the Ka'ba, advised people to perform two rakaat prayers at night to assist against the fear and loneliness of the grave.

The Prophet states that the best of you is one whose words are good and proper, feeds the hungry, and while others are asleep, recites the Night Prayers.

The Prophet three times said to Imam Ali⁽ᵃ⁾ – Upon you is the Night Prayer:

عليك بصلاة اليل،

عليك بصلاة اليل،

عليك بصلاة اليل.

Imam Sādiq؏ states the ornament and pride of the believer is the recitation of the Night Prayer. Someone said to Imam Ali؏ I have been deprived from the recitation of the Night Prayer, Imam Ali؏ replied:

قيّدتك ذنوبك

Your sins have tied you up.

Imam Sādiq؏ states that the Prophet۞ in his Witr prayer[1], would seek forgiveness 70 times over.[2]

Rising Early and Night Vigil

{إِنَّ نَاشِئَةَ اللَّيْلِ هِىَ أَشَدُّ وَطْئًا وَأَقْوَمُ قِيلًا}

Surely the first part of the night is heavier in tread, more upright in speech (Al Muzzammil 73:6).

Allah۞ has sworn an oath on all parts of the day: I swear by: The Dawn, The Morning, The Day, The Afternoon, but has done so thrice with regards to Dawn

{وَاللَّيْلِ إِذَا يَسْرِ}

By the night when it journeys on!

{وَاللَّيْلِ إِذَا عَسْعَسَ}

By the night swarming

{وَاللَّيْلِ إِذْ أَدْبَرَ}

And the night when it retreats

The oath in the above three Ayāt is an oath by the night as it ends.

And with regards to seeking forgiveness at dawn and rising early, two Ayāt have been revealed

---

[1] The final supplication of the Night Prayer.

[2] (تهذيب الاحكام Tahdhib al-Ahkam) V2 P120

{وَالْمُسْتَغْفِرِينَ بِالْأَسْحَارِ}

Imploring God's pardon at the daybreak.

{وَبِالْأَسْحَارِ هُمْ يَسْتَغْفِرُونَ}

And in the mornings they would ask for forgiveness

Allah۞ says to Moses۞ Oh Moses, a liar is he who claims he loves Me but while when the night falls, instead of conversing with Me, he falls asleep.

The Prophet۞ states that two rakāt in the heart of the night is more beloved to me than the world and everything that's in it.

Lesson 10 The Two Forgotten Obligations

First: Islamic Tax (Zakāt)

{إِنَّمَا ٱلصَّدَقَتُ لِلْفُقَرَآءِ وَٱلْمَسَكِينِ وَٱلْعَمِلِينَ عَلَيْهَا وَٱلْمُؤَلَّفَةِ قُلُوبُهُمْ وَفِي ٱلرِّقَابِ وَٱلْغَرِمِينَ وَفِي سَبِيلِ ٱللَّهِ وَٱبْنِ ٱلسَّبِيلِ فَرِيضَةً مِّنَ ٱللَّهِ وَٱللَّهُ عَلِيمٌ حَكِيمٌ}

The freewill offerings (Zakāt) are for the poor and needy, those who work to collect

them, those whose hearts are brought together, the ransoming of slaves, debtors, in

God's way, and the traveller; so God ordains; God is All-knowing, All-wise.

(Tawba 9:60).

The commandment for Zakāt came down in Mecca, however due to the very few Muslims and limited wealth for the giving of Zakāt, people would pay themselves. After the forming of the Islamic government in Medina, Zakāt was collected from people and placed in the Islamic Treasury (*Bayt-ul-Māl*) and the wealth was concentrated under the control of an Islamic governor.

{خُذْ مِنْ أَمْوَالِهِمْ صَدَقَةً}

Take of their wealth a freewill offering (Tawba 9:103).

Zakāt is not specific to Islam, rather was also a present in religions prior to it. Prophet Jesus said in his cradle:

{وَأَوْصَانِي بِالصَّلَاةِ وَالزَّكَاةِ}

and He has enjoined me to pray, and to give the alms (Maryam 19:31).

And Prophet Moses﷿ stated Bani Israel

{وَأَقِيمُوا الصَّلَاةَ وَآتُوا الزَّكَاةَ}

And perform the prayer, and pay the alms (Al Baqarah 2:43).

And with regards to Prophethood in general, we read

{وَجَعَلْنَاهُمْ أَئِمَّةً يَهْدُونَ بِأَمْرِنَا وَأَوْحَيْنَا إِلَيْهِمْ فِعْلَ الْخَيْرَاتِ وَإِقَامَ الصَّلَاةِ وَإِيتَاءَ الزَّكَاةِ}

And appointed them to be leaders guiding by Our command, and We revealed to them the doing of good deeds, and to perform the prayer, and to pay the alms (Ambiyā 21:73).

In the Qur'ān, four expressions have been used for Zakāt:

1. Giving of one's wealth.

{وَآتَى الْمَالَ عَلَى حُبِّهِ ذَوِى الْقُرْبَى}

To give of one's substance, however cherished, to kinsmen. (Al Baqarah 2:177).

2. Freewill offering (Al Tawbah 9:103, see above)
3. Expend

{يُقِيمُوا الصَّلَاةَ وَيُنفِقُوا}

They perform the prayer, and expend (Abraham 14:31).

4. Zakāt.

{يُقِيمُونَ الصَّلَاةَ وَيُؤْتُونَ الزَّكَاةَ}

perform the prayer and pay the alms (Al Māidah 5:55).

The Importance of Zakāt

Generally, in the Holy Qur'ān Zakāt comes alongside prayer and there is no other obligatory deed that has been so strongly associated with prayer. According to narrations, the condition in which prayers are accepted are the payments of Zakāt. This relationship delivers the link between the connection with Allahﷻ and the connection with people.

It is forbidden for Sa'ada[1] to receive Zakāt, when a group of people from Bani Hashim[2] requested from the Prophetﷺ that they be in charge of collecting the Zakāt of cattle, and from that be able to be paid a portion of the Zakāt for their collection work, the Prophetﷺ stated that Zakāt is forbidden upon you and I, unless it be that both the recipient and giver are both Sa'ada.

The law of Zakāt is not for Islam to be inclined towards having a group of poor people be recipients while the rich be donors, but rather is a solution to an outside problem in society. The rich are also afflicted with such phenomena as theft, fire, collisions, war and captivity, and in the Islamic system there must be a budgetary measure for social security.

In the narrations, it says that Allahﷻ has placed a certain amount of wealth in the hands of the rich for the purpose of solving the problems of the poor and if it is known that this was insufficient, the wealth would be increased for them. If the rights of the poor are all paid to them the lives of all will be good and if the rich paid the Zakāt of the poor, there would be no existence of poverty[3].

Contrary to the beliefs of some with regards to limiting the growth of individual income and limiting its growth, Islam believes that we must give a proportion of our freedom so that mankind struggles to work hard, initiates, and reaps the rewards, the rewards naturally grow, but also to pay taxes in the same vein. The condition of paying the Zakāt "in the way of Allahﷻ" is not just for the poor, but for any cause that will assist the sovereign line of Islam.

For the sake of saving society from the evil of the wicked, we can use Zakāt to our benefit and this spending would be considered part of "Softening of the Hearts[4]" spending.

---

[1] Sa'ada are people who are linked to the Holy Prophetﷺ through paternal linkage.
[2] Who themselves are Sa'ada.
[3] (Wasa'il Al Shia وسائل الشيعة) V6 P4
[4] المؤلفة القلوبهم

If someone has upon their neck a blood money debt to pay which they cannot pay, this can be considered "Debt"[1] and Zakāt money can be used to assist them.

Perhaps the term "Upon the necks"[2] can also be considered part of Zakāt spending towards freeing prisoners and securing their expenditure.

The spending of Zakāt need not be equally distributed amongst its allowable expenditure, but rather, can be at the discretion of the Islamic jurist and be distributed according to the needs and necessities.

Zakāt is a means of adjusting the distribution of wealth.

Zakāt, is an act of thankfulness to the divine blessings.

Zakāt, diminishes socio-economic classes and removes hatred between the rich and the poor.

Zakāt develops the soul of generosity and mercy in mankind and reduces material desires and dependence.

Zakāt is the bankroll to the security of the deprived in society. To the poor it says – don't worry, to the bankrupt it says – renew your efforts, to the traveller it says – don't be afraid of becoming stranded, to the workers it says – your share is protected, and to the slaves - it gives the promise of freedom, it booms the market for the divine mercy and the hearts of others are attracted to Islam.

Neglecting Allah, human exploitation, hard heartedness, tyranny and debauchery, is the fruit of rivalry in worldly matters and wealth, while Zakāt is the medicine for this disease.

Zakāt, as well as reducing deprivation, it orientates others towards Islam or at least it prevents leaning towards working with the enemies of Islam. Just as noted in the narrations, sometimes those with weak faith can have their faith made firm through a little financial help and by being closer to Islam.

Zakāt, being part of the schematic of the Islamic system, is the foundation of societal justice, elimination of poverty, security for workers, international popular relations, freedom of slaves and the imprisoned, movement of

---

[1] والغارمين

[2] و فى الرقاب

potential energy and protecting the religion and royalty of Muslims and the spread of its services in general.

Second: Khums

According to narrations and the Shia belief, Ayah 41 of Surah Al Anfāl covers all forms of income broader than business, work, and trade and one source of khums has been mentioned in this Ayah while others have been mentioned in the narrations.

$$\{وَاعْلَمُوا أَنَّمَا غَنِمْتُم مِّن شَيْءٍ فَأَنَّ لِلَّـهِ خُمُسَهُ\}$$

Know that, whatever booty you take, the fifth of it is God's

(Al Anfāl 8:41).

Khums, in the narrations, is of such importance that it is said that anyone who does not pay Khums of their wealth, their wealth is not lawful to them and they are not allowed to utilise their wealth, and the clothes worn in prayers which has not had its khums paid is problematic.

The jurists have identified seven items in which khums needs to be paid on:

1. Profit and benefits of business and annual income
2. Treasure
3. Minerals
4. Gem stones obtained through sea-diving
5. Unlawful wealth mixed with lawful wealth
6. Land purchased by a non-warring disbeliever buys from a Muslim
7. Spoils of War[1]

It's clearly obvious that Allah is not in need of khums, but rather Allah's portion is to be used for the governance of Allah's Law and the government of the Prophet, propagation and deliverance of the call of Islam to the ears of the world, saving those who are oppressed and weak and preventing corruption.

Based on narrations, Gods portion is under the authority of the Prophet along with the Prophets share, and after him, under the authority of the Imam. And these are, during the time of occultation, under the authority of the specified representatives of the general representatives of the Imam,

---

[1] (Tafsir Safi تفسير الصافي)

meaning the jurist with all the conditions fulfilled, and the jurisprudential judge.

Of other spending that khums can be utilised for as per the narrations, the impoverished and those stranded in travel, on the heirs of Bani Hashim as it is forbidden for impoverished Saadaat to receive Zakāt, they are able to utilise the khums stream of funds to secure their needs[1]. In fact, Islam has made obligatory two things which would eradicate poverty in society: The first is Zakāt which is in relation to all societies poor, and the other is khums, part of which has been dedicated to the needy Sa'ada, and both khums and Zakāt payable is to be as much as one years' worth of their needs, no more.

---

[1] (Wasa'il Al Shia وسائل الشيعة) V6 The Chapter of Khums

Lesson 11 The Father and The Mother

{وَقَضَىٰ رَبُّكَ أَلَّا تَعْبُدُوا إِلَّا إِيَّاهُ وَبِالْوَالِدَيْنِ إِحْسَانًا إِمَّا يَبْلُغَنَّ عِندَكَ الْكِبَرَ أَحَدُهُمَا أَوْ كِلَاهُمَا فَلَا تَقُل لَّهُمَا أُفٍّ وَلَا تَنْهَرْهُمَا وَقُل لَّهُمَا قَوْلًا كَرِيمًا وَاخْفِضْ لَهُمَا جَنَاحَ الذُّلِّ مِنَ الرَّحْمَةِ وَقُل رَّبِّ ارْحَمْهُمَا كَمَا رَبَّيَانِي صَغِيرًا}

Thy Lord has decreed you shall not serve any but Him, and to be good to parents, whether one or both of them attains old age with thee; say not to them 'Fie' neither chide them, but speak unto them words respectful, and lower to them the wing of humbleness out of mercy and say; 'My Lord, have mercy upon them, as they raised me up when I was little.' (Al Isrā 17:23-24).

In narrations, with regards to being good to parents, much advice has been given while hurting them is disapproved of:

The reward of a merciful look towards your parents is the acceptance of pilgrimage. Their approval is Divine approval and their anger is Allah's anger. Goodness towards the father and the mother extends one's life and becomes the cause of our own children's goodness towards us.

In the narrations, it is said that even if they strike you, do not say "fie", don't give them disobedient look, do not raise your hand, do not walk ahead of them, do not call them by their names, do not do anything which may cause enmity from people towards them, do not sit before they do and assist them in their needs before they request assistance.

A man who was carrying his mother on his shoulders for the circumambulation during pilgrimage saw the Prophet at that moment, and asked; Have I filled my obligation towards my mother? The Prophet replied, you have not even fulfilled your obligation in return for a single moan she cried during your childbirth!

In narrations, it is stated that even if the parents hit their own children, the children should say "May God forgive you", the words which are the very same "respectful words".

The Prophet was asked if there were good deeds for the parents after their passing away? He replied affirmatively, reciting prayers for them and seeking forgiveness on their behalf, fulfilling their commitments, paying for the misdeeds and respecting their friends.

A man complained to the Prophet about his father. The Prophet sought the father and when questioned, the old man said there was a day when I was strong and wealthy and assisted my children, but today he is the wealthy one and does not assist me. The Prophet cried and stated there is no stone nor sand that heard this story and did not weep, then said to the son, you and everything you own is your fathers.

Goodness towards parents is of the characteristics of the Prophets. As Prophet Jesus was characterised as "وَبَرًّا بِوَالِدَتِي" (to cherish my mother)[1] and Prophet Yahya as "وَبَرًّا بِوَالِدَيْهِ" (and cherishing his parents[2]).

If parents are aware such is the case that the Holy Qur'ān advises us to be good to parents after monotheism, it would stimulate life in to invite their own children to monotheism.

So, we can derive some points from this Ayah:

1. Serving parents and goodness towards the father and mother is a character of a true monotheist. - *you shall not serve any but Him, and to be good to parents.*

---

[1] Holy Qur'ān Surah Maryam 19:32
[2] Holy Qur'ān Surah Maryam 19:14

2. The order of kindness towards parents is like the order of monotheism, definite, and never to expire. – *decreed.*
3. Goodness towards parents comes next to monotheism and obedience to Allah to point out that this deed is not only an intellectual and humane obligation, but also a religious one - *Thy Lord has decreed you shall not serve any but Him, and to be good to parents.*
4. The new generation must, under the shadow of faith, have a strong relationship with the past generations - *you shall not serve any but Him, and to be good to parents.*
5. In goodness towards parents, being a Muslim is not a condition [meaning even if parents are not Muslim]- *and to be good to parents.*
6. In goodness to the father and mother, there is no differentiation between the two - *and to be good to parents.*
7. Do good to your parents without an intermediary and with your own hands - *be good to parents.*
8. Doing good is higher than spending and includes showing love, politeness, teaching, consultation, obedience, thankfulness, attention, and the like - *be good to parents.*
9. Goodness towards parents has no borders or limits - *be good to parents.* (Unlike the poor, where the obligation is until satiety is reached, and jihad, where it is only required until sedition is lifted, and fasting where it is only until dusk sets in.)
10. The Holy Qur'ān's advice to do good is directed at the offspring, not parents - *be good to parents.* That's because parents are naturally good and kind to their children and no advice is needed as such.
11. The more physical and psychological need the parents have, the stronger the obligation is to do good towards them - *whether one or both of them attains old age.*
12. A healthy father and mother should not be sent to a nursing home, but rather need to be looked after nearby - *with thee.*
13. Both good action and polite and good speech is required - *be good... speak unto them words respectful.*
14. With regards to doing good towards parents and generous words, there is no condition for anything in return. That means even if they do not return the generosity, you still need to fulfil your obligation, speaking well and doing good.

15. Under all circumstances, and in all their perfection, needs to stay humble towards their parents and not to show off their perfection - *and lower to them the wing of humbleness.*

16. Humility with regards to parents must be out of kindness and love, not superficial and made up, or for the sake of their wealth - *and lower to them the wing of humbleness out of mercy.*

17. Children must with regards to their parents be not only humble, but also seek mercy for them on their behalf from Allah﷾ - *My Lord, have mercy upon them.*

18. The supplication of the child for their parents is one that is answered, otherwise, Allah﷾ would not have given the command to supplicate for them - and say; *'My Lord, have mercy upon them'.*

19. Supplication for the father and mother is a Divine order and a sign of gratitude towards them - say; *'My Lord, have mercy upon them'.*

20. The mercy of Allah﷾ is in return for the pain and trouble parents go through in raising children - *'My Lord, have mercy upon them, as they raised me up...'.* Sometimes Allah﷾ says to the offspring; do not be regretful of your own mercy, and seek help from Allah﷾, for one is never able to discharge their obligation towards them.

21. Do not forget your past, the hard times and the problems your parents bore for your sake during your childhood and tender years - *as they raised me up.*

22. The father and mother must raise their children based upon love - *have mercy upon them, as they raised me up.*

23. One must be thankful and show their gratitude towards their tutors - *have mercy upon them, as they raised me up.*

In Ayāt 83 of Surah Al Baqarah, 36 of An Nisā, 151 of An A'am, and 23 of Al Isrā, advice has been given to do good to your parents, but in Ayah 14 of Surah Luqmānﷵ, goodness towards parents has been given in the shape of divine advice:

$$\{وَوَصَّيْنَا الْإِنسَانَ بِوَالِدَيْهِ\}$$

And We have charged man concerning his parents (Luqmān 31:14).

Yes, respect towards parents is a human right, not an Islamic one, an eternal right, not a seasonal or temporary one.

In the narrations, we read that goodness towards parents is an obligation under all circumstances, be it they are bad or good, be it they are dead or alive.

The Prophet was seen to be more respectful towards his sister[1] than towards his brother through breastfeeding, when asked for the reason why, he said that because she showed more respect towards her mother[2].

We read in the Holy Qur'ān that both Prophets Jesus and Yahya were ordered to show respect towards their parents.[3]

The Prophet states that after the prayers at the peak of their time, a deed better than respect towards parents does not exist[4].

An Extension of The Meaning of Parents

In the Islamic culture, your heavenly guide, teacher, tutor and father-in-law can all be coined the term father. In some narrations, the Prophet and Imam Ali are known as the fathers of the Islamic Nation.

أنا وعلى أبوا هذه الأمة

Ali and I are the fathers of this nation.

Just as Prophet Ibrahīm is considered the father of the Arabs –

{مِّلَّةَ أَبِيكُمْ إِبْرَاهِيمَ}

being the creed of your father Abraham (Al Hajj 22:78).

In the final days of the Prophets life while he was on his nurse bed, he said to Imam Ali , to go to the people and say with a loud voice –

- May Allah's curse be upon anyone who is disobedient to their parents
- May Allah's curse be upon any slave that runs away from their master

---

[1] This refers to his sister in whom he shared a wet nurse with rather than a biological sister from the same parents.
[2] (Al Kafi) V2 P118
[3] Holy Qur'ān Maryam 19:14 and 32.
[4] (Mizan Al-Hikmah ميزان الْحِكمة)

—   May Allah's﷾ curse be upon anyone who does not pay the right of the worker and whom they hire

Imam Ali؏ left and stated these words amongst the people then returned. Some of the companions thought this advice to be simple and plain, and wondered: The advice regarding parents and masters and workers was previously heard, it's not a new message for it to be sent to us from the messengers nursing bed.

The Prophetﷺ, realising the people did not comprehend the depth of the message, sent Imam Ali؏ back to the people with a follow up message, asking him to say that what was meant by disobedience to parents, is disobedience to the Divine Guide. Oh Ali؏, you and I are the Fathers of this Nation and one who escapes from us, gives cause to receive Allah's﷾ anger. You and I have become hired to guide these people and anyone who does not pay the right of the hired gives cause to receive of Allah's﷾ anger.

In this incident, an observation is made that though goodness and obedience towards parents is one apparent and official meaning, yet in Islam, the issue is a much wider one.

Lesson 12 Thankfulness and Gratitude

{وَإِذْ تَأَذَّنَ رَبُّكُمْ لَئِن شَكَرْتُمْ لَأَزِيدَنَّكُمْ.وَلَئِن كَفَرْتُمْ إِنَّ عَذَابِى لَشَدِيدٌ}

And when your Lord proclaimed, "If you are thankful, surely I will increase you, but if you are thankless My chastisement is surely terrible."' (Ibrahīm 14:7).

Imam Sādiq states that gratefulness towards blessings is far from sin. He also stated gratitude is where one knows their blessings are from Allah (and not know their blessings as being a result of their cleverness, knowledge, mind and efforts or of others) and is content with what has been given to them from Allah, and those very blessings should not be used as a means to sin, true gratitude is when one uses the blessings of Allah in the way of Allah.

Gratitude for divine blessings are many, and cannot be listed.

We read in the narrations that Allah inspired to Prophet Moses, to deliver my (Allahs) right of gratitude, Prophet Moses replied that he could not possibly do so, as each word to thank itself requires another thanks. The inspiration came down… that that very confession you make and that you know everything is from Me, is the best way to thank me.[1]

---

[1] (Tafseer-e-Namoona)

Gratitude towards others is gratitude towards Allah, it has been brought to us through narrations that: Anyone who is not thankful of the created, is not thankful of Allah.

مَن لَم يَشْكُرِ المُنعِمَ مِنَ المَخلُوقِينَ لَم يَشكُرِ اللهَ عَزَّوَجَلَّ[1]

If the blessings of Allah are spent in a way contrary to the rights in which it must be spent in, that shows ingratitude and is the foundation of blasphemy. *"If you are thankless"*, or as in another Ayah "those *who exchanged the bounty of God with unthankfulness*"[2], are those who exchanged the blessings from Allah in to blasphemy.

Thanking Allah

Allah has no need for our worship and gratitude and the Holy Qur'ān has repeatedly indicated and stated this: Allah is all sufficient and not in need of you.[3] But our attention towards him is our capital for our own honour and growth, just as the sun is not in need of us, we benefit from its sunlight.

One of the praises that Allah has of Prophets is their spirit of gratitude. For example, Prophet Noah, because of all his patience and perseverance in the face of an unfaithful wife, children and people, Allah in the Holy Qur'ān recognises his gratitude and knows him as being thankful:

{إِنَّهُ كَانَ عَبْدًا شَكُورًا}

He was a thankful servant (Al-Isrā 17:3).

Many times, Allah complains from many people for their (lack of) gratitude.

Of course, the grace of gratitude is one that one must be sought from Allah, just like Prophet Sulaimān requested the same:

{رَبِّ أَوْزِعْنِي أَنْ أَشْكُرَ نِعْمَتَكَ الَّتِي أَنْعَمْتَ عَلَيَّ}

My Lord, dispose me that I may be thankful for Thy blessing wherewith Thou

hast blessed me. (An Naml 27:19).

---

[1] (Bihar Al Anwar بحار الأنوار) V71 P44
[2] Holy Qur'ān Ibrahīm 14:28
[3] See Surahs An Naml 24:40 and Luqmān 31:12

"Dispose me" means to ask Allah to inspire, make me attached to, and to love, being thankful towards Your blessings. We are mostly aware of and thankful for the blessings that we deal with on a daily basis, and are negligent of many blessings, such as the blessings that have come to us through inheritance and good people, or the thousands of calamities that have been prevented from befalling us, and the spiritual blessings such as faith in Allah and His Guides, or the dislike of blasphemy and debauchery and sin, such as how Allah reminds us in the Qur'ān:

{اللَّـهَ حَبَّبَ إِلَيْكُمُ الْإِيمَانَ وَزَيَّنَهُ فِي قُلُوبِكُمْ وَكَرَّهَ إِلَيْكُمُ الْكُفْرَ وَالْفُسُوقَ وَالْعِصْيَانَ}

God has endeared to you belief, decking it fair in your hearts, and He has made detestable to you unbelief and ungodliness and disobedience. (Al Hujarāt 49:7).

As well as that which has been mentioned, some of the supplications of the Divinely Guided concentrate on the blessings of Allah and show gratitude and gives thanks for them, so that the spirit of gratitude is brought to life and strengthened.

Thanking Allah is sometimes with the tongue and through speech, and sometimes through action and deed. In the narrations, we read that every time we are thoughtful of a blessing from the Divine blessings, in gratitude to it one should prostrate upon the earth, and even if we are riding on a horse, we come down and do this and if we can't, we put our forehead (in prostration) on the higher part of the saddle, and if we can't do that either, we place our forehead (in prostration) on our hand and be thankful of Allah.[1]

Examples of Practical Gratitude

1. Prayer, is the best form of gratitude to Allah. Allah says to His Prophet:

{إِنَّا أَعْطَيْنَاكَ الْكَوْثَرَ}

Surely We have given thee abundance;

{فَصَلِّ لِرَبِّكَ وَانْحَرْ}

So pray unto thy Lord and sacrifice.

---

[1] (Al Kafi) – Chapter of Gratitude V25

2. Fasting, just as gratitude was shown by the Prophets of Allah towards Him for their blessings through fasting.[1]

3. Serving the people. The Holy Qur'ān states that if an illiterate person asks a literate person to write a letter, the literate person should not turn the request down in gratitude to the blessing of literacy and write the letter.

{وَلَا يَأْبَ كَاتِبٌ أَن يَكْتُبَ كَمَا عَلَّمَهُ اللَّـهُ}

And let a writer write it down between you justly, and let not any writer refuse to write it down, as God has taught him. (Al Baqarah 2:282).

Here, writing a letter in the service of people is a form of gratitude to the blessing of literacy.

4. Contentment. The Prophet states that

وَكُنْ قَنِعًا تَكُنْ أَشْكَرَ النَّاس

Be content and you will be the most gratuitous of the people.[2]

5. Take care of orphans. Allah says to the Prophet, in gratitude to you being sheltered as an orphan, do not oppress an orphan:

{فَأَمَّا الْيَتِيمَ فَلَا تَقْهَرْ}

As for the orphan, do not oppress him. (Ad Dhuhā 93:9)

6. Assisting the deprived and the needy. Allah says to the Prophet, in gratitude to you having been in need and I made you needless, do not scold the needy that requests your assistance:

{وَأَمَّا السَّائِلَ فَلَا تَنْهَرْ}

And as for the beggar, scold him not. (Ad Dhuha 93:9).

7. Gratitude towards others. Allah says to the Prophet, In gratitude and incentive to those who pay Zakāt, send your praise towards them, for your praise brings tranquillity to them:

---

[1] (Wasa'il Al Shia وسائل الشيعة) V10 P446

[2] (Mustadrak al-Wasā'il مستدرك الوسائل) V11 Hadith 12,676

{وَصَلِّ عَلَيْهِمْ إِنَّ صَلَاتَكَ سَكَنٌ لَّهُمْ}

And pray for them; thy prayers are a comfort for them. (Al Tawba 9:103).

Gratitude in The Face of Hardship

The Holy Qur'ān states

{وَعَسَىٰ أَن تَكْرَهُوا شَيْئًا وَهُوَ خَيْرٌ لَّكُمْ وَعَسَىٰ أَن تُحِبُّوا شَيْئًا وَهُوَ شَرٌّ لَّكُمْ}

Yet it may happen that you will hate a thing which is better for you; and it may

happen that you will love a thing which is worse for you. (Al Baqarah 2:216).

If we knew, others have more problems.

If we knew, problems increase our attention towards Allah.

If we knew, problems break our vanity and gets rid of hard heartedness.

If we knew, problems remind us of those afflicted with ill fate.

If we knew, problems bring our thoughts to defence and initiative.

If we knew, problems remind us of our previous blessings.

If we knew, problems are the atonement of our sins.

If we knew, problems are the reason for reward in the hereafter.

If we knew, problems are a warning to us and the alarm that awakens us to resurrection.

If we knew, problems are the reason we become acquainted with patience or know who our real friends are.

And if we knew, it could be that greater problems or harder ones may befall us, whereby we would recognise although our problems are externally bitter, they can be sweet in the right place. Yes, for children, dates are sweet but onions and hot pepper are avoided, while for mature, grown parents who have foresight, the benefits of both sour and sweetness are known.

Imam Ali, during the War of Uhud, states that fighting in the battlefield is a blessing that we must be thankful for it.[1] And his daughter, Zainab,

---

[1] (Nahjul Balagha) Speech 156.

responding to the felonious Bani Umayya stated with regards to Karbala[1] – I saw nothing but beauty.[2]

---

[1] Karbala is the site in which Imam Husain, the brother of Syeda Zeinab, son of Imam Ali۩ and Sayyida Fātima and grandson۩ of the Prophet was massacred along with 72 companions.

[2] (Bihar Al Anwar بحار الأنوار) V45 P116

Lesson 13 Divine Delegates
Animals Are Divine Delegates

{ فَلَمَّا قَضَيْنَا عَلَيْهِ الْمَوْتَ مَا دَلَّهُمْ عَلَى مَوْتِهِ إِلَّا دَابَّةُ الْأَرْضِ تَأْكُلُ مِنسَأَتَهُ فَلَمَّا خَرَّ تَبَيَّنَتِ الْجِنُّ أَن لَّوْ كَانُوا يَعْلَمُونَ الْغَيْبَ مَا لَبِثُوا فِي الْعَذَابِ الْمُهِينِ }

And when We decreed that he should die, naught indicated to them that he was dead but the Beast of the Earth (termites) devouring his staff; and when he fell down, the jinn saw clearly that, had they only known the Unseen, they would not have continued in the humbling chastisement. (Seba 34:14).

Many times, in the Qur'ān, the role and delegation given to animals has been demonstrated. As examples:

1. Part of a sacrificed cow (The Cow of Bani Israel) brought back to life a murdered man to bear witness as to who killed him.

{إِنَّ اللَّـهَ يَأْمُرُكُمْ أَن تَذْبَحُوا بَقَرَةً}

'God commands you to sacrifice a cow.' (Al Baqarah 2:67)

2. A spider that protected the Prophetﷺ while he was in the cave.

{إِلَّا تَنصُرُوهُ فَقَدْ نَصَرَهُ اللَّـهُ}

If you do not help him, yet God has helped him already (Al Tawba 9:40).

81

3. A crow became the teacher of man.

{فَبَعَثَ اللَّـهُ غُرَابًا }

Then God sent forth a raven (Al Māida 5:31).

4. A hoopoe bird that was assigned to deliver the letter of Prophet Suliman ﷺ to Queen Bilqīs, the ruler of the Land of Shība:

{اذْهَب بِّكِتَابِي هَـٰذَا}

Take this letter of mine.(An Naml 27:28).

5. Small birds that were charged with the task of throwing stones upon the Army of the Elephant:

{وَأَرْسَلَ عَلَيْهِمْ طَيْرًا أَبَابِيلَ}

And He sent upon them birds in flights (Al Fīl 105:3).

6. A serpent, a means for truth for Prophet Moses ﷺ:

{فَإِذَا هِيَ ثُعْبَانٌ مُّبِينٌ}

and behold, it was a serpent manifest. (Al A'rāf 7:107).

7. A whale, commissioned to punishment for Prophet Yunus ﷺ:

{فَالْتَقَمَهُ الْحُوتُ}

Then the whale swallowed him down (As Saffāt 37:142).

8. Termites, the means in which the death of Prophet Sulaiman ﷺ was discovered:

{دَابَّةُ الْأَرْضِ تَأْكُلُ مِنسَأَتَهُ}

The Beast of the Earth devouring his staff. (Seba 34:14).

9. The dog, a companion of the people of the cave, was responsible for guarding them:

{وَكَلْبُهُم بَاسِطٌ ذِرَاعَيْهِ بِالْوَصِيدِ}

and their dog 'stretching its paws on the threshold. (Al Kahf 18:18).

10. Four birds (Peacock, pigeon, cock, and crow) provided contentment to Prophet Ibrahīm☘:

$$\{فَخُذْ أَرْبَعَةً مِّنَ الطَّيْرِ\}$$

Take four birds. (Al Baqarah 2:260).

11. A donkey, the reason for certainty of Prophet Uzair☘ in the Resurrection:

$$\{وَانظُرْ إِلَى حِمَارِكَ\}$$

And look at thy donkey. (Al Baqarah 2:259).

12. The camel, cow, and sheep in the Hajj Pilgrimage, become divine symbols:

$$\{وَالْبُدْنَ جَعَلْنَاهَا لَكُم مِّن شَعَائِرِ اللَّهِ\}$$

And the beasts of sacrifice -- We have appointed them for you as among God's waymarks (Al Hajj 22:36).

13. Animals, become a means to know God:

$$\{أَفَلَا يَنظُرُونَ إِلَى الْإِبِلِ كَيْفَ خُلِقَتْ\}$$

What, do they not consider how the camel was created? (Al Ghāshiya 88:17).

14. Animals, become a means of a test to mankind:

$$\{تَنَالُهُ أَيْدِيكُمْ وَرِمَاحُكُمْ\}$$

that your hands and lances attain (Al Māida 5:94).

15. Animals, become the miracles of God:

$$\{هَٰذِهِ نَاقَةُ اللَّهِ\}$$

This is the She-camel of God. (Al Arāf 7:73).

16. Animals, are a means of Divine anger and punishment:

$$\{وَالْجَرَادَ وَالْقُمَّلَ وَالضَّفَادِعَ\}$$

The locusts, the lice and the frogs (Al Arāf 7:133).

84

Lesson 14 All That is Sacred in Islam

Respecting All That Is Sacred In Islam

{يَـٰٓأَيُّهَا ٱلَّذِينَ ءَامَنُوا لَا تَرْفَعُوٓا أَصْوَٰتَكُمْ فَوْقَ صَوْتِ ٱلنَّبِيِّ وَلَا تَجْهَرُوا لَهُۥ بِٱلْقَوْلِ كَجَهْرِ بَعْضِكُمْ لِبَعْضٍ أَن تَحْبَطَ أَعْمَٰلُكُمْ وَأَنتُمْ لَاتَشْعُرُونَ}

O believers, raise not your voices above the Prophet's voice, and be not loud in your speech to him, as you are loud one to another, lest your works fail while you are not aware. (Al-Hujurāt 49:2).

With all the different principles and beliefs, the respective elders of each group are respected in a special way. Cities, streets, universities, airports, schools and organisations are named after such people. Likewise, in Islam, individuals and even some plants and inanimate objects are considered sacred.

In Islam, the roots of what is sacred and great is linked to its relationship with Allahﷻ Himself and the stronger that relationship, the more sacred and greater they become, and we must give and protect the respect due to them. However, note that with regards to being sacred:

1. Allahﷻ is the source of all sacredness and polytheists that equate others with God, will on the day of resurrection confess to their deviation and say to their imaginary idols – the secret of our

85

misfortune is our equating you (the idols) with the Lord of the Worlds:

$$\{ \text{إِذْ نُسَوِّيكُم بِرَبِّ ٱلْعَٰلَمِينَ} \}$$

When we made you equal with the Lord of all Being (Ash Shu'arā 26:98)

In the Qur'ān, the glorification and perfection of Allah۞ is repeated often, which means we must respect and sanctify Allah۞ where we recognise that it cannot even be imagined that Allah۞ has an iota of imperfection or shortcoming. Not only Allah۞ in His nature, but His name is also pure:

$$\{ \text{سَبِّحِ ٱسْمَ رَبِّكَ ٱلْأَعْلَى} \}$$

Magnify the Name of thy Lord the Most High. (Al A'lā 87:1).

2. The book of Allah۞ is also sacred and respected. When Allah۞ knows the Holy Qur'ān as Great:

$$\{ \text{وَٱلْقُرْآنَ الْعَظِيمَ} \}$$

And the Mighty Qur'ān (Al Hijr 15:87).

We must therefore know the Holy Qur'ān as Great, and when the Holy Qur'ān is known (Holy Qur'ān 56:77), we must then revere it, and since the Holy Qur'ān is praiseworthy (Qur'ān 50:1), we must therefore praise it.

3. The rights of the Divine Guides, all of the Prophets and their successors and especially that of the Prophet۞ and his Purified Household, have been given a special status which in the aforementioned Surah[1], the respect they deserve has partly been mentioned such as not going ahead of them, not raising or voice to be louder than theirs, and in other Ayāt, to send our praises to the Prophet۞.

---

[1] Al-Hujurāt 49:2

{إِنَّ ٱللَّهَ وَمَلَٰئِكَتَهُۥ يُصَلُّونَ عَلَى ٱلنَّبِيِّ يَٰأَيُّهَا ٱلَّذِينَ ءَامَنُوا صَلُّوا عَلَيْهِ وَسَلِّمُوا تَسْلِيمًا}

God and His angels bless the Prophet. O believers, do you also bless him, and pray him peace. (Al Ahzāb 33:56).

Of course, it must be noted that after the passing of the Prophet, the above respect will also apply to and for visitation of the Prophets resting place, and to the resting places of his Purified Household﷽, and Progeny, and those who have taken his place, and everyone around him who are associated with him, especially the scholars and just jurists and the religious authorities, as per narrations, those who are in place of the Prophet﷽, all deserve our utmost respect. In the narrations it is stated that anyone who refutes a just jurist says, is like the one who refutes what the Purified Household﷽, of the Prophet﷽ have said, and one who refutes what they have said, is like one who refutes what Allah﷽ says.[1]

Not only the Prophets in person, but what is linked to them also has sanctity and greatness. In the Holy Qur'ān we read

{وَقَالَ لَهُمْ نَبِيُّهُمْ إِنَّ ءَايَةَ مُلْكِهِۦ أَن يَأْتِيَكُمُ ٱلتَّابُوتُ فِيهِ سَكِينَةٌ مِّن رَّبِّكُمْ وَبَقِيَّةٌ مِّمَّا تَرَكَ ءَالُ مُوسَىٰ وَءَالُ هَٰرُونَ تَحْمِلُهُ ٱلْمَلَٰئِكَةُ إِنَّ فِي ذَٰلِكَ لَءَايَةً لَّكُمْ إِن كُنتُم مُّؤْمِنِينَ}

And their Prophet said to them, 'The sign of his kingship is that the Ark will come to you, in it a Shechina from your Lord, and a remnant of what the folk of Moses and Aaron's folk left behind, the angels bearing it. Surely in that shall be a sign for you, if you are believers.'(Al Baqarah 2:248).

The basket that Prophet Moses'﷽ placed him in when she sent floating, was used after his death to place the tablets and scrolls and of what was with him in terms of prophetic miracles and the belongings of his offspring. The chest was so sacred that the Angels would carry it and then bring it back to lead them to victory against an evil powerful tyrant.

---

[1] (Bihar Al Anwar بحار الأنوار) V27 P238

4. In Islam, the parents have a special sanctity and greatness associated with them. In the Qur'ān, monotheism precedes respecting and doing good to the parents five times and showing gratitude towards them is placed next to showing gratitude to Allah.

{أَشْكُرْ لِي وَلِوَالِدَيْكَ}

'Be thankful to Me, and to thy parents. (Luqmān 31:14).

Respecting the parents is to the point where looking at them with the look of love and respect is considered worship and we are advised to not raise our voices above theirs, and if we go on a trip that causes harm to them is prohibited, and prayers during that travel must be prayed in full (not shortened).

5. In Islam, certain periods of time, such as the Night of Power, some places, such as Mosques, some rocks, such as the Black Stone, some waters, such as Zam-Zam, some soil, such as the soil of Imam Husain, some clothes, such as the pilgrimage clothing, are considered sacred and special respect must be duly given to them. Prophet Moses in respect of the "Valley of Moses" took off his footwear when he entered:

{فَٱخْلَعْ نَعْلَيْكَ إِنَّكَ بِٱلْوَادِ ٱلْمُقَدَّسِ طُوًى}

Put off thy shoes; thou art in the holy valley, Towa.

(Tāhā 20:12).

The Holy Mosque of Mecca is considered sacred and non-Muslims have no right to enter it

{إِنَّمَا ٱلْمُشْرِكُونَ نَجَسٌ فَلَا يَقْرَبُوا ٱلْمَسْجِدَ ٱلْحَرَامَ}

The idolaters are indeed unclean; so let them not come near the Holy Mosque. (At Tawba 9:28).

Places of worship and mosques are sacred and when we go to such places, we should go clean and well presented.

{خُذُوا زِينَتَكُمْ عِندَ كُلِّ مَسْجِدٍ}

Take your adornment at every place of worship.

(Al A'rāf (7:31).

And anyone who is in a state of uncleanliness or impurity (Junub) has no right to pause in a mosque:

{وَلَا جُنُبًا إِلَّا عَابِرِى سَبِيلٍ حَتَّىٰ تَغْتَسِلُوا}

Or defiled -- unless you are traversing a way -- until you have washed yourselves

(An Nisā 4:43).

The Mosque is of such an honourable status that such people as Abraham, Ismael, Zakariyah and Maryam, may peace and blessings be upon them all, were charged with the responsibility of purifying them:

{طَهِّرَا بَيْتِىَ}

Purify My House (Al Baqarah 2:125).

Even the mother of Maryam, who thought she was carrying a son, swore her child to serving the Al Aqsa Mosque

{إِنِّى نَذَرْتُ لَكَ مَا فِى بَطْنِى مُحَرَّرًا}

Lord, I have vowed to Thee, in dedication, what is within my womb. (Āle Imrān 3:35).

6. A person with belief also has sanctity and greatness, so much so that the honour of the believer is more than the honour of the Ka'baa and the persecution and backbiting them is prohibited and defending their right is obligatory, and even after death, it is prohibited to exhume the grave.

Insulting The Prophetﷺ, Allah'sﷻ Defence

بِسْمِ ٱللَّـهِ ٱلرَّحْمَـٰنِ ٱلرَّحِيمِ

إِنَّآ أَعْطَيْنَـٰكَ ٱلْكَوْثَرَ ﴿١﴾ فَصَلِّ لِرَبِّكَ وَٱنْحَرْ ﴿٢﴾

إِنَّ شَانِئَكَ هُوَ ٱلْأَبْتَرُ ﴿٣﴾

In the Name of God, the Merciful, the Compassionate

Surely We have given thee abundance; so pray unto thy Lord and sacrifice. Surely

he that hates thee, he is the one cut off (Al-Kawthar 108:1-3).

The stronger the attack on religion and what is sacred in it, the stronger the defence must be. There were many bold attacks upon the Prophet☽, accused as a sorcerer, fortune teller, poet and possessed, all of which were rebuffed in the Holy Qur'ān. He was told that he was possessed by jinn, but Allah☽ says:

﴿مَآ أَنتَ بِنِعْمَةِ رَبِّكَ بِمَجْنُونٍ﴾

Thou art not, by the blessing of thy Lord, a man possessed.

(Al Qalam 68:2).

He was told that he was not a messenger of God, for which Allah☽ states:

﴿إِنَّكَ لَمِنَ ٱلْمُرْسَلِينَ﴾

Thou art truly among the Envoys (messengers) (Yā Sīn 36:3).

He was accused of being a poet possessed, but Allah☽ states:

﴿وَمَا عَلَّمْنَـٰهُ ٱلشِّعْرَ وَمَا يَنبَغِى لَهُ﴾

We have not taught him poetry; it is not seemly for him.

(Yā Sīn 36:69).

To that individual, an Ayah was revealed:

﴿إِنَّ شَانِئَكَ هُوَ ٱلْأَبْتَرُ﴾

Certainly, he who insults you is the one who is cut off.

(Al Kawthar 108:3)

Indeed, the answer to the one who insults the best of creations as being "cut off", is to be given Kawthar, and then everyone's eyes were bedazzled, and everyone's mind was awed.

For the last Ayah of Surah Al-Kawthar (108:3), we understand that Kawthar is the opposite of "cut off".

The Prophet was mocked as being one who is "cut off"[1], but Allah states in the Holy Qur'ān "he is the one cut off" (Al-Kawthar 108:3).

"Cut off" is a term used by Arabs to describe one who is left with no heir because of having no sons, and with their death, they leave no trace behind. "Kawthar" in this Surah is used as an answer to that mockery, and the best evidence of it are the twelve Divinely Guided leaders from Sayyida Fātima(sa), the daughter of the Prophet.

Of course, "Kawthar", or as translated "Abundance", has a general meaning and includes every abundant good, but not every abundance is "Kawthar". The Holy Qur'ān states:

{فَلَا تُعْجِبْكَ أَمْوَالُهُمْ وَلَا أَوْلَادُهُمْ إِنَّمَا يُرِيدُ اللَّهُ لِيُعَذِّبَهُم بِهَا فِي الْحَيَوٰةِ الدُّنْيَا وَتَزْهَقَ أَنفُسُهُمْ وَهُمْ كَافِرُونَ}

So let not their possessions or their children please thee; God only desires thereby to chastise them in this present life, and that their souls should depart while they are unbelievers (Al Tawba 9:55).

During the events of the liberation of Mecca, in which the disbelievers entered Islam in waves and waves, Allah gives the single order of glorification:

{وَرَأَيْتَ النَّاسَ يَدْخُلُونَ فِي دِينِ اللَّـهِ أَفْوَاجًا فَسَبِّحْ}
When comes the help of God, and victory, then glorify (An Nasr 110:2-3).

But in return for being given "Kawthar", Allah states to the Prophet:

{فَصَلِّ لِرَبِّكَ وَانْحَرْ}
so pray unto thy Lord and sacrifice (Al Kawthar 108:2).

Indicating the provision of "Kawthar" is more significant than the waves of disbelievers entering Islam.

---

[1] Having no surviving son to be his heir.

Lesson 15 Migration

Migration For the Sake Of Religious Attainment

{وَمَا كَانَ الْمُؤْمِنُونَ لِيَنفِرُوا كَافَّةً فَلَوْلَا نَفَرَ مِن كُلِّ فِرْقَةٍ مِّنْهُمْ طَائِفَةٌ لِّيَتَفَقَّهُوا فِي الدِّينِ وَلِيُنذِرُوا قَوْمَهُمْ إِذَا رَجَعُوا إِلَيْهِمْ لَعَلَّهُمْ يَحْذَرُونَ}

It is not for the believers to go forth totally; but why should not a party of every section of them go forth, to become learned in religion, and to warn their people when they return to them, that haply they may beware? (At-Tawba 9:122).

To become learned in religion means to strive for the attainment of a deep and meaningful understanding of the religion, its fundamental beliefs and jurisprudence. Sometimes, this goal can be for worldly desires, social status, a desire to learn, to argue, debate and for amusement. And so as not to fall behind with regards to friends, and sometimes it is for the sake of religion itself, for Allah, paradise and for the sake of saving the Nation of Islam. The above Ayah recognises the latter as the one of value, where they warn their people and invite them to the path of Allah "that haply they may beware"… The Prince of the Believers Imam Ali advised his child "Be Learned in religion for the learned are the inheritors of the Prophets"[1]. Imam Husain,

---

[1] (Bihar Al Anwar بحار الأنوار) V1 P216

on the night of Ashura, Praised Allah﷾ in sentences such as Praise Allah﷾ that has made me learned in religion.[1]

Imam Sādiqﷺ was asked what to do if something happens to the Imam, to which he replied with the above Ayah and the advice that from each city and each group of people some must act for the sake of knowing their Imam.[2]

Individuals from each location must go to religious center points for the sake of attaining religious knowledge and return to their own locations until such time that all locations have enough religious scholars to satisfy that area's needs. Yes, migration is an inherent part of faith. Migration should be either for the defense of religion, or for acquiring religious knowledge. Therefore, the acquisition of knowledge in religion and then passing on the knowledge and teaching the people of one's birthplace is an obligation that is lifted from the rest if fulfilled by others. So, for the students of Islamic Seminaries, there are two obligatory migrations, one is from their hometown towards the Islamic Seminaries and learning centers, and the other from those centers back to their own homeland. So, remaining in Islamic Seminaries, with the exceptions of the teachers themselves, is not permitted.

Of course, acquiring this knowledge is not just about jurisprudence, but all of the sciences related to religion and able to be researched, in detail and in depth… "to become learned in religion."

Religious knowledge is of value where the scholar is aware of the times and surroundings and of the devilish ways and tactical strategies of the enemy so that they can warn and make aware. In that way the speech of one Islamic scholar can be relied upon… to become learned… to warn their people (it is possible to have one scholar per area, that would be enough as proof to act upon).

Scholars must go after people and not wait for their invitation "when they return to them" and not wait for everyone's unwavering support and following because a group of people from every area will never accept the path of religion and God – "that haply they may beware".

---

[1] (موسوعة كلمات الامام)

[2] (Tafsīr Nūr al-Thaqalayn - تفسير نور الثقلين)

The Historic Migration of The Prophet ﷺ

{إِنَّ الَّذِينَ آمَنُوا وَهَاجَرُوا وَجَاهَدُوا بِأَمْوَالِهِمْ وَأَنفُسِهِمْ فِي سَبِيلِ اللَّـهِ وَالَّذِينَ آوَوا وَّنَصَرُوا أُولَـٰئِكَ بَعْضُهُمْ أَوْلِيَاءُ بَعْضٍ وَالَّذِينَ آمَنُوا وَلَمْ يُهَاجِرُوا مَا لَكُم مِّن وَلَايَتِهِم مِّن شَيْءٍ حَتَّىٰ يُهَاجِرُوا}

Those who believe and have emigrated and struggled with their possessions and their selves in the way of God, and those who have given refuge and help -- those are friends one of another. And those who believe but have not emigrated -- you have no duty of friendship towards them till they emigrate... (Anfāl 8:72).

In the thirteenth year after the Revelation and after ten years of public invitation to Islam by the Prophet ﷺ, the disbelievers of Mecca have not yet stopped harming and persecuting the Prophet ﷺ and Muslims, and day by day they increased the persecution against them until they conspired to kill the Prophet ﷺ and destroy Islam from its roots.

With the Prophets ﷺ knowledge and the self-sacrifice and devotion of Imam Ali ؏, a night was prepared for the migration of the Prophet ﷺ and the Prophet ﷺ, on the first of the month of Rabi' Al-awwal, began his journey towards a cave called "Thawr"[1] and by way of miracle, stayed hidden there for three days. During that period only Imam Ali ؏ brought him food and news from outside.

In the end, the Prophet ﷺ advised Imam Ali ؏, based on the announcement of the migration of Muslims to Yathrib and bringing his family along with him, continued his journey towards Yathrib and after travelling approximately 400 kilometers arrived in Quba on the 12th day of Rabi' Al-awwal and the rest of the migrants also continued to arrive in Quba.

The people of Yathrib prepared for the coming of the Prophet ﷺ and migrants to their city and greeted them with open hearts. The name of the city was changed from Yathrib to Madinat Al Nabi and Madinat Al Rasool[2]. At the point, in order to prevent and distance the city from division, the Prophet ﷺ paired up the approximately three hundred migrants and Ansar[3] as brothers

---

[1] Literally means "Bull"

[2] Meaning the City of the Prophet| and the City of the Messenger.

[3] Ansar are what the people of Yathrib are referred to upon accepting the migrants.

and poured brotherhood upon them, and the base for the first Masjid of Islam was founded and Masjid Quba was built.

The migrants are those that believed in the Prophetﷺ in Mecca and because they were under considerable pressure there, they left their homes and belongings in Mecca to join the Prophet in the migration and the Ansar are the Muslims of Medina that gave the Prophetﷺ and the migrants a place amongst them and supported them.

Generally, nations mark the most important events faced in their social, scientific, and religious history and know it as a conjunctive to the narrative of their history, such as the birth of the Messiah for Christians, or the Year of the Elephant (the year in which the army of Abraha from Yemen attacked Mecca but were divinely annihilated) to the Arabs, both examples having set the beginning of the year.

From the point of view that the religion of Islam is the most complete and comprehensive heavenly religion and at the same time is independent of all other religions, and so Muslims did not mark the beginning of their calendar with the birth of the Messiah, nor with the Year of the Elephant notwithstanding it was the same year in which the Prophetﷺ was born. Not even the year in which the Revelation came down upon the Prophetﷺ was marked as the start of the Islamic history. But the migration to Medina in which an independent Islamic government was formed and Muslims were able at that point to act freely, the Prophetﷺ personally declared the Hijri calendar. As such we can derive from "from the first day" in the Ayah

{لَّمَسْجِدٌ أُسِّسَ عَلَى ٱلتَّقْوَىٰ مِنْ أَوَّلِ يَوْمٍ أَحَقُّ أَن تَقُومَ فِيهِ

فِيهِ رِجَالٌ يُحِبُّونَ أَن يَتَطَهَّرُوا وَٱللَّهُ يُحِبُّ ٱلْمُطَّهِّرِينَ}

A mosque that was founded upon godfearing from the first day is worthier

for thee to stand in; therein are men who love to cleanse themselves; and

God loves those who cleanse themselves. (Al Tawba 9:108).

As being the building of Masjid Quba as well as being for the foundation for the Hijri year as the first action taken by the Prophetﷺ in the migration was the building of Masjid Quba. Indeed, if it was not for the migration, most, if not all of Islam, would have been limited and destroyed.

Of course, in the dawn of Islam two migrations were faced: One in the fifth year after the Revelation in which a group of Muslims migrated to Ethiopia, and the other in the 13ᵗʰ Year after Revelation, the migration from Mecca to Medina.

The Effects and Blessings of Migration

Most of the disasters that befall us are a result of drowning ourselves in creature comforts and leaving migration that is the source of building foundations. If all the great Muslim minds, experts and professionals that are in the west migrate back to their own countries, not only is it a blow to the enemy but also a cause of strength for Islam and Islamic nations.

Migration is not limited to the Prophetﷺ, but rather migration from an environment of disbelief, idol worship, and sin, for the salvation of religion, faith and for leaving the environment of disobedience to Allahﷻ, is obligatory. So in answer for those who give the excuse of unhealthy environment for their polluted self and perpetration of sin, the reply will be that *Was not Gods Earth large enough for you to migrate elsewhere…?:*

{كُنَّا مُسْتَضْعَفِينَ فِي ٱلْأَرْضِ قَالُوا أَلَمْ تَكُنْ أَرْضُ ٱللَّهِ وَاسِعَةً}

'We were abased in the earth.' The angels will say, 'But was not God's earth wide…'(An Nisā 4:97).

Of course, with attention to the term "abased", it becomes apparent that if one is able to uphold the good and forbid the evil, that one must carry that obligation out and not leave that society in order to repair it.

Imam Sādiq؏ states that if you live on a land in which there is disobedience of Allahﷻ, migrate from there to another land.

إذا عصي الله في أرض أنت فيها فاخرج منها إلى غيرها[1]

So, migration for the purpose of obtaining knowledge and migration for the sake of distributing one's knowledge to others are both obligatory.

---

[1] (Bihar Al Anwar بحار الأنوار) V19 P35

Lesson 16 Exegesis of Surah Qadr

بِسْمِ ٱللَّهِ ٱلرَّحْمَٰنِ ٱلرَّحِيمِ

إِنَّآ أَنزَلْنَٰهُ فِى لَيْلَةِ ٱلْقَدْرِ ﴿١﴾ وَمَآ أَدْرَىٰكَ مَا لَيْلَةُ ٱلْقَدْرِ ﴿٢﴾ لَيْلَةُ ٱلْقَدْرِ خَيْرٌ مِّنْ أَلْفِ شَهْرٍ ﴿٣﴾ تَنَزَّلُ ٱلْمَلَٰٓئِكَةُ وَٱلرُّوحُ فِيهَا بِإِذْنِ رَبِّهِم مِّن كُلِّ أَمْرٍ ﴿٤﴾ سَلَٰمٌ هِىَ حَتَّىٰ مَطْلَعِ ٱلْفَجْرِ ﴿٥﴾

In the Name of God, the Merciful, the Compassionate - Behold, We sent it down on the Night of Power; And what shall teach thee what is the Night of Power? The Night of Power is better than a thousand months; in it the angels and the Spirit descend, by the leave of their Lord, upon every command. Peace it is, till the rising of dawn. (Al Qadr 97:1-5).

The term "Qadr – قدر" in the Holy Qur'ān is used to mean a number of things:

A) Status and position, such as in the following Ayah:

{وَمَا قَدَرُوا ٱللَّـهَ حَقَّ قَدْرِهِۦٓ}

They measured not God with His true measure.

(Al Ana'ām 6:91).

B) Estimation and decree, such as in the following Ayah:

{جِئْتَ عَلَى قَدَرٍ يَٰمُوسَىٰ}

Then you came hither (to this sacred place), Moses, according to a decree. (Tā Hā 20:40).

C) Constriction and difficulty, such as in the following Ayah:

{وَمَن قُدِرَ عَلَيْهِ رِزْقُهُ}

As for him whose provision is stinted to him. (At Talaq 65:7).

The first two meanings are suitable for the term commonly translated as "Night of Power" (97:1), such as elsewhere in the Holy Holy Qur'ān where it states, with regards to that night,

{فِيهَا يُفْرَقُ كُلُّ أَمْرٍ حَكِيمٍ}

Therein every wise bidding. (Ad Dukhān 44:4).

Therefore, the "Night of Power" is not restricted to the night in which the Holy Qur'ān descended nor to the time of the Prophet☀, but rather every Holy month of Ramadhān there is a Night of Power in which the affairs of the year ahead through to the next Night of Power is determined.

Staying awake and keeping vigil on that night with supplication and prayers and reciting the Holy Qur'ān is the advice given to us by the Prophet☀ and the Ahlul Bayt and is considered to be one of three nights – the night of the 23rd of the holy Month of Ramadhān being the one of most certainty.   A person asked the Prophet☀ that, due to the great distance from his house to the city, to advise him of which one night to come to the city (in the month of Ramadhān), to which his Holiness replied… come to the city on the Night of the 23rd.[1]

Imam Sādiq☀, while he was ill, requested he be taken to the mosque on the night of the 23rd.[2] While Sayyida Fātima al Zahra÷ on this night, would keep her children awake by sprinkling water on their faces.[3]

---

[1] (Wasa'il Al Shia وسائل الشيعة) V3 P307
[2] (Bihar Al Anwar بحار الأنوار) V95 P169
[3] (Bihar Al Anwar بحار الأنوار) V94 P10

It has also come in to narrations that the Prophet⸢ﷺ⸣ would pack up his bed in the last ten nights of the Holy month of Ramadhān and keep vigil those ten nights.[1]

In a long narration from the Prophet⸢ﷺ⸣ we read that Prophet Moses⸢as⸣ implored Allah⸢swt⸣ for nearness... to which the reply was

قربى لمن استيقظ ليلة القدر

Nearness to Me is keeping vigil on the Night of Power.

He asked: Oh Nurturer, I implore your Mercy. The Answer, My Mercy is for those who were merciful to the needy on the Night of Power.

رحمتى لمن رحم المساكين لىلة القدر

He said: O My Lord, I seek permission to cross upon the Straight Path. The Answer: That is for those who give alms on the Night of Power.

ذلك لمن تصدق بصدقة فى ليلة القدر

He said: My Lord, I seek the trees of paradise and its fruits. The reply: that is for those who glorified a glorification on the Night of Power.

ذلك لمن سبح تسبيحه فى ليلة القدر

He said: My Lord, I seek to be rescued from the Hellfire. The Answer: That is for those who sought forgiveness on the Night of Power.

ذلك لمن استغفر فى ليلة القدر

In the end, he said: My Lord, I seek your satisfaction. The reply: My satisfaction is for those who prayed two raka'at prayers on the Night of Power.

رضاي لمن صلى ركعتين في ليلة القدر[2]

One of the strangest realities of history is the striking of Imam Ali⸢as⸣ on the Night of Power, in which he was in the sanctuary of worship and in the state of prayers. Yes, the most honourable of Gods creations, in the most

---

[1] (Majmaul Bayan Fi Tafsir Al-Quran مجمع البيان فى تفسير القرآن)

[2] (Wasa'il Al Shia وسائل الشيعة) V8 P20

honourable of places, in the most honourable of time and in the most honourable state, was martyred.

The length of time the Night of Power is a complete night on Earth which takes up 24 hours, not that it is particular to a specific place such as Mecca where a night may be for eight hours. Just as the Celebration of the end of Ramadhān, Eid Al Fitr, is a complete 24-hour cycle that every part of the world participates in.

Perhaps the comparison of the Night of Power for mankind with that of the Holy Qur'ān descending to earth is a symbol of the relationship between mankind's decree and the Holy Qur'ān. If one follows the Holy Qur'ān, it leads to happiness and redemption, and if one is distant from it, it leads to adversity and misery for them.

Abu Dhar says: I asked the Prophet if the Night of Power was for the times of the Prophets and if it was for them and that after they departed the world, that the Night of Power and the descent that occurs on that night stops? To which he replied: The Night of Power will continue through to the Day of Resurrection.

Perhaps the secret behind which night is actually the Night of Power is so that people can keep Vigil on more than just the one night, for someone who keeps vigil one night does not become so proud and for the one who missed a night, does not become hopeless.

It has been stated in traditions that a good deed on the Night of Power is better than a good deed of a thousand months without the Night of Power.[1]

The decree on the Night of Power is with the decent and presence of angels:

$$\{تَنَزَّلُ ٱلْمَلَٰٓئِكَةُ وَٱلرُّوحُ فِيهَا بِإِذْنِ رَبِّهِم مِّن كُلِّ أَمْرٍ\}$$

In it the angels and the Spirit descend, by the leave of their Lord, upon every

command.

The meaning of Peace in this Surah is that of favour blessings from Allah upon his worshippers on this night who seek security, mercy and blessings and seek to close the doors of curse and punishment, as the whisperings of

---

[1] (Man la yahduruhu al-Faqih من لا يحضره الفقيه) V3 P158

Satan in those nights have no effect. In the Night of Power, angels descend on earth and send their greetings upon every man and woman that is in the state of worship. Just as in the Day of Resurrection where the people of heaven are greeted with a "Salam":

﴿سَلَـٰمٌ عَلَيْكُمْ طِبْتُمْ فَٱدْخُلُوهَا خَـٰلِدِينَ﴾

'Peace be upon you! Well you have fared; enter in, to dwell forever.' (Az Zumar 39:73).

The Angels in The Holy Qur'ān

1. Angels are the honoured servants (Holy Qur'ān 21:26).
2. Infallible and submissive to Allah﷾ (Holy Qur'ān 66:6)
3. The running of certain affairs is in their hands (Holy Qur'ān 79:5, 51:4)
4. Are watchful and vigilant as to what humans speak and say (Holy Qur'ān 50:18).
5. Are the writers of the books of those in the world (Holy Qur'ān 43:80).
6. Are the givers of good tidings to the warriors of war on the battlefield, providing the good tidings of answers to prayers and news of offspring and the good tidings to the believers at the moment of death (Holy Qur'ān 9:40, 19:7, 41:30).
7. Are ordered to punish a divine punishment to the criminals (Holy Qur'ān 11:77).
8. Are the protectors of mankind (Holy Qur'ān 6:61).
9. Ask forgiveness for those who believe (Holy Qur'ān 40:7).
10. Provide intercession (Holy Qur'ān 53:26).
11. Curse the disbelievers (Holy Qur'ān 2:161).
12. Rescuers of battlefield warriors (Holy Qur'ān 3:125).
13. Punish criminals at the time of their death (Holy Qur'ān 8:50).
14. Greet those heavenly bound (Holy Qur'ān 13:24).
15. Are responsible for punishment in Hell (Holy Qur'ān 74:30).
16. Are responsible for taking the souls (Holy Qur'ān 6:61).
17. Have class and position (Holy Qur'ān 37:164).
18. Responsible for the bringing down of revelation (Holy Qur'ān 16:2).
19. Sometimes appear in the form of human (Holy Qur'ān 19:17).
20. Are tireless worshippers (Holy Qur'ān 41:38).

21. Also communicate with those who are not Prophets (Holy Qur'ān 19:19).
22. Some angels are selected over others (Holy Qur'ān 22:75).
23. Faith for angels is a must (Holy Qur'ān 2:285, 4:136).

It has come in narrations that one should protest those who reject the "Imams" with Surah Al Qadr, because on the basis of this Surah, angels descend upon the earth every year. At a time when the Prophetﷺ was on this earth, they would come down with his presence, however, after his passing upon whose presence will they descend?

It is clear that not everyone can host the heavenly angels and one who does, must be like the Prophetﷺ, divinely guided and guardian of the matters of mankind, and he is no other than a Divinely Guided Imam for which in our time, is the Honourable Mahdi ﷻ and angels descend upon earth on the Night of Power in his presence.

Lesson 17 Allah's Decrees

Types Of Decrees

{يَمْحُوا ٱللَّهُ مَا يَشَاءُ وَيُثْبِتُ وَعِندَهُۥٓ أُمُّ ٱلْكِتَٰبِ}

God blots out, and He establishes whatsoever He will; and with Him is the
Essence of the Book. (A'rāf 13:39).

Based on the Ayāt of the Holy Qur'ān and narrations, the Divine Decrees are
of two types:

The first, matters that have an eternal benefit, and so its laws are also eternal.
Such as the Ayāt

{مَا يُبَدَّلُ ٱلْقَوْلُ لَدَيَّ}

The Word is not changed with Me (Qāf 50:29).

{وَكُلُّ شَىْءٍ عِندَهُۥ بِمِقْدَارٍ}

Everything with Him has its measure (Ar R'ad 13:8).

Everything has a detailed register of accounts with the Lord and as such, the
Divine Decrees are recorded in a guarded tablet[1] and only the nearest to
Allah and with His permission can have knowledge of it.

---

[1] {فِى لَوْحٍ مَّحْفُوظٍ} - in a guarded tablet (Al Burūj 85:22)

{كِتَـٰبٌ مَّرْقُومٌ يَشْهَدُهُ ٱلْمُقَرَّبُونَ}

A book inscribed, witnessed by those brought nigh. (Al Mutaffifīn 83: 20-21).

The second, are matters which are not definite and their benefits depend upon the actions and behaviours of the people, such as repentance from sins which has the benefits of forgiveness, or alms giving which has the benefits of repelling calamities, or oppressions which brings about Divine Wrath upon the sinners. So, Allah is not hand tied with the matters revolving around the administration of all his creation, and with His eternal wisdom and knowledge that He has, he can change some conditions to change the creations and the laws with in it. It is clear that these changes are not a result of ignorance or a change in view, or even regret on His part, but rather, it is based on His wisdom and the changed conditions and/or end of that period in question.

The Holy Qur'ān with regards to this presents many examples, some of which are:

1. Supplicate to me, I will answer you (Holy Qur'ān 40:60). Mankind, can with supplication, bring about benefits to himself and change his own denouement.
2. Allah's rules are not fixed everywhere, perhaps Allah, upon the fulfilling the necessary conditions, will rewrite a new program and bring something new to pass (Holy Qur'ān 65:1).
3. He has a specific status for every specific day (Holy Qur'ān 55:29).
4. Because some people choose a deviated path, Allah leads their hearts astray (Holy Qur'ān 61:5).
5. With faith and piety, Divine Wrath changes to Divine kindness and blessings (Holy Qur'ān 7:96).
6. Allah will not change the direction of any nation unless they change themselves (Holy Qur'ān 13:11).
7. One who repents, believes, and performs a good deed, Allah will change that individual's bad deeds into good (Holy Qur'ān 19:60).
8. If you return, We too shall return (Holy Qur'ān 17:8).

Of course, Allah's knowledge is based on the foundation of cause and effect, in such a way that He knows that if one uses a particular method, a particular result will occur, and the use of another method results in an alternative outcome.

What is a New Manifestation?

In Shia Islam, New Manifestations (بداء) is something that becomes apparent that we, contrary to its reality, suspected, not a change in the knowledge of Allah and the discovery of contradiction for Allah.

New Manifestation in creation, is like a law that supersedes an older one, just as we thought that a particular law was eternal… yet later realise that it has changed. Of course, this does not point to a regretful lawmaker or their ignorance, but rather the changed conditions that brought about changes in laws. The correct prescription the doctor writes remains correct so long as the condition of the patient is unchanged… but once it changes, a new prescription needs to be written.

Here, we present some examples of New Manifestations in the Holy Qur'ān:

1. We suspected that Allah ordered Prophet Ibrahīm to slaughter his son, wanting his son Ismael dead and his blood scattered on the earth. Yet later it becomes apparent that the will of Allah in this matter was a test of the father, not of the slaughter.
2. We suspected that the promise of Allah with Prophet Moses consisted of a period of thirty-night period, but then realise that it was always intended to be forty nights (Holy Qur'ān 7:142), but was divided in to two periods in the form of a test, the first being thirty, the latter being a further ten nights.
3. We suspected that the direction for which Muslims will face to pray will always be that of Al- Quds, but then Ayāt were revealed changing the direction eternally to the House of Allah, The Ka'ba.
4. Once the signs of Divine Wrath started to appear, even Prophet Yunus was sure that the punishment was coming and his disbelieving nation would be annihilated, and so left his people. But then the nation started to believe and the Divine Wrath was lifted (Holy Qur'ān 10:98).

At any rate, New Manifestation does not implicate change in His knowledge or ignorance, as Allah knew from the outset the blood of Ismael would not be shed by his father, the period of litany for Prophet Moses was always going to be forty nights, the direction to which Muslims eternally pray towards will be the Ka'ba and the Nation of Yunus will be saved. Yet the style and syntax in which the stories are narrated may give a superficial impression otherwise.

So, it was not a change in His knowledge, but our view of the story in a new light.

New Manifestations have a specific role in cultivating lessons, one of which is that one, until the last moment in their life, must maintain hope in the changing conditions, the spirit of reliance upon Allah should be brought to life, not become a slave to the apparent outlook and faith in the unseen and Allah's ability increased. One must make an effort with repentance, alms giving, litany and supplication until the way of events and Divine Wrath are changed for the better.

Lesson 18 The Purified Household عليهم السلام

The Ayah of Purification

{إِنَّمَا يُرِيدُ ٱللَّهُ لِيُذْهِبَ عَنكُمُ ٱلرِّجْسَ أَهْلَ ٱلْبَيْتِ وَيُطَهِّرَكُمْ تَطْهِيرًا}

God only desires to put away from you, the People of the Household, abomination and to cleanse you. (Al Ahzāb 33:33).

The term إِنَّمَا (translated as "only") here indicates that this Ayah is most certainly restricted in relation to only this particular Household عليهم السلام, Divinely Purified.

The term يُرِيدُ (translated as "desires") is an Existential Will[1], because the will of Allah ﷻ in the legislative sense is that all mankind should be purified.

The term ٱلرِّجْسَ (translated as "abomination") relates to any impurity, apparent or internal.

The term أَهْلَ ٱلْبَيْتِ عليهم السلام (translate as "People of the House عليهم السلام") are not all the members of the Prophets ﷺ family, but of certain members whose names have been mentioned in both Shia and Sunni references. They are Imam Ali, Sayyida Fātima Zahra, Imam Hasan and Imam Husain عليهم السلام

---

1 اراده تکوینی

Question: What is the basis of this restriction? And why is it that this part of the Ayah is not in relation to all of the Prophetsﷺ wives and house members?

Answer One: Narrations from the Prophetsﷺ wives themselves, even from Aisha and Um Salma who asked the Prophetﷺ if they were members of the Purified Household؏؟ To which the Prophetﷺ replied in the negative.

Two: We read in multiple narrations that the Prophetﷺ placed a cloak over those five members of the Household؏, of whom one was the Prophetﷺ himself, and stated that these are the members of My Household؏ and no one else has permission to enter it.

Three: The Prophetﷺ, to establish the exclusivity of the five members of the Purified Household؏, would pass by the home of Sayyida Fātima Zahra﷐ for six months (or eight, or nine months in some narrations) for the dawn prayers and state the words:

الصلاة يا اهل البيت إِنَّمَا يُرِيدُ ٱللَّه لِيُذْهِبَ عَنكُمُ ٱلرِّجْسَ أَهْلَ ٱلْبَيْتِ وَيُطَهِّرَكُمْ تَطْهِيرًا

Time for Prayers, oh People of the Household؏, God only desires to put away from you, the People of the Household؏, abomination and to cleanse you.

In the book *Restoration of The Truth* by Al-Hilli[1], more than seventy narrations from well-respected Sunni sources were identified that identify this Ayah as one that is specific to those five members of the Purified Household؏, and in the well-respected book[2], over 130 narrations based upon these foundations are narrated.[3] [4]

In any case, this Ayah does not encapsulate the wives of the Prophetﷺ because:

They were sometimes caught up in sin. In Surah At-Tahrim, we read that the Prophetﷺ confided in with some of his wives with a secret but the trust was breached with the secret being told to another. This, in the Holy Qur'ān was identified as a sin:

---

[1] علامه حلی :احقاق الحق

[2] شواهد التنزیل

[3] (Tafseer-e-Namoona)

[4] (Tafsīr Nūr al-Thaqalayn - تفسیر نور الثقلین)

{إِن تَتُوبَآ إِلَى ٱللَّهِ فَقَدْ صَغَتْ قُلُوبُكُمَا}

If you two repent to God, yet your hearts certainly inclined. (At Tahrīm 66:4).

Aisha, a wife of the Prophet, initiated the War of the Camel against Imam Ali and later regretted her actions, for many Muslims were killed in battle.

Answering Doubts

1. Doesn't "cleanse you "implicate that the Purified Household were impure to start and then Allah cleansed and purified them?

   A precondition to purification is not to be impure, as the Holy Qur'ān states, the Houris[1] are described as purified, whereas they have not committed an ounce of sin. Likewise, to "cleanse you" here is to keep them purified and guard them from all impurities, not to cleanse them of previous sins.

2. If this Ayah is with regards to only five people, why is it amongst an Ayah relating to the wives of the Prophet?

   A) The part of the Ayah starting with "*God only desires*" was revealed separately from the Ayah in which it is found, however, it was placed within that particular ayah while the Holy Qur'ān was being collated.

   B) In the Exegesis of Majamaa' Al Bayān, it is explained that the poets, writers and eloquent speakers would commonly state something new and important in between other sentences in order to maximise its effect. Just as in the new bulletin when the reporter breaks his sentence to say something such as "We have breaking news… or with news just in…", this gives a sort of mental shock to the listener promoting the news item.

   The view of this Ayah is that of Surah Māida, Ayah 3, that discusses issues relating to guardianship, leadership and perfection of religion and all of the blessings and seeking the satisfaction of Allah, and the despair for the unbelievers, while being in relation to a revelation describing amongst other items pork meat and blood. This is a secret of its compilation which safeguarded the Holy Qur'ān from the hands of the non-

---

[1] Beautiful, big, and lustrous eyed partners… rewarded to the believers in the heaven.

believers. Just as when women may hide their jewellery inside their pillow filling when they leave their homes, not because gold has anything to do with cotton, but because they want to guard themselves from the hands of the thieves.

C) In the middle of the Ayah advising the wives of the Prophetﷺ, all of a sudden, the Ayah changes tone towards the Purity of the Purified Household؏, effectively saying: O wives of the Prophetﷺ, you are living amongst a household whom are Divinely Guided and Purified, so you must have greater care and attention to your piety for sure.

D) When it comes to the Purified Household؏... the pronoun used is collectively for majority male persons, contrary to when discussing the wives Prophetﷺ, the pronoun used was collective feminine.

Part of The Household؏ or Not?
In the Holy Qur'ān, Allahﷻ states

$$\{قَالَ يَا نُوحُ إِنَّهُ لَيْسَ مِنْ أَهْلِكَ إِنَّهُ عَمَلٌ غَيْرُ صَالِحٍ\}$$

He said: "O Noah! He is not of thy family: For his conduct is unrighteous. (Hud

11:46).

While many narrations from the Prophetﷺ and Ahlul Bay that have reached us start with "Not of us are they who…". For example, the Prophet ﷺ stated

$$من غشَّ مسلماً فليس منا$$

Whoever cheats another Muslim is not of us.

Elsewhere it is narrated he said whoever respects another out of fear is not of us. While it has also been narrated the Prophetﷺ stated

$$من أصبح ولم يهتم بأمور المسلمين، فليس بمسلم$$

Whoever wakes up in the morning without giving thought as to how they can serve the Islamic Nation, is not a Muslim.

Elsewhere, the traditions narrate a friend of the Prophetﷺ is one who is submissive to Allahﷻ, even if he has no relation with the Prophetﷺ, while his enemy is one who is non-submissive to Allah☉, regardless of how close he was to the Prophet☉

Lesson 19 Love for The Ahlul Bayt

{قُل لَّآ أَسْـَٔلُكُمْ عَلَيْهِ أَجْرًا إِلَّا ٱلْمَوَدَّةَ فِى ٱلْقُرْبَىٰ

وَمَن يَقْتَرِفْ حَسَنَةً نَّزِدْ لَهُۥ فِيهَا حُسْنًا إِنَّ ٱللَّهَ غَفُورٌ شَكُورٌ}

Say 'I do not ask of you a wage for this, except love for the kinsfolk; and whosoever gains a good deed, We shall give him increase of good in respect of it. Surely God is All-forgiving, All-thankful. (Ash Shura 42:23).

The Holy Qur'ān shows us this kind of position multiple times, which the Prophets seek nothing of rewards or wages from the people. In Surah Ash Shura from Ayāt 100 to 180, this kind of statement from different Prophets^ is repeated. Likewise, the Prophet☷ also did not seek any materialistic compensation, but twice in the Holy Qur'ān from he was ordered by Allah☷ with the statement "Say" to seek a spiritual compensation that will benefit the people themselves.

This spiritual compensation itself comes in the form of two phrases. In one instance, it comes in the following terms:

{قُلْ مَآ أَسْـَٔلُكُمْ عَلَيْهِ مِنْ أَجْرٍ إِلَّا مَن شَآءَ أَن يَتَّخِذَ إِلَىٰ رَبِّهِۦ سَبِيلًا}

Say: 'I do not ask of you a wage for this, except for him who wishes to take to his Lord a way.' (Al Furqān 25:57).

And in another form, as stated in the Ayah at the start of this lesson. And in the following Ayah we see that the benefit of the spiritual compensation being sought is for the people themselves:

{قُلْ مَا سَأَلْتُكُم مِّنْ أَجْرٍ فَهُوَ لَكُمْ إِنْ أَجْرِىَ إِلَّا عَلَى ٱللَّهِ وَهُوَ عَلَىٰ كُلِّ شَىْءٍ شَهِيدٌ}

Say: 'I have asked no wage of you; that shall be yours. My wage falls only upon God; and He is witness over everything.' (Saba 34:47).

So the Prophet ﷺ announces that if I was to seek any compensation and ask for you to love my kinship, the Purified Household, it is for the reason that the benefit of this will fall back to yourselves. Because anyone who has a close relationship with the Purified Household, will be followers and supporters of the Purified Household and anyone who is a proactive supporter of the Divinely Guided will be following the path of Allah.

"*...except for him who wishes to take to his Lord a way*", is like the example of a teacher that says to their students I seek nothing from you but that you study the subject well, a benefit that will go back to the students themselves. So therefore, the reward of the message is two: One is to choose to follow the Path of Allah and the other is for the Love of the kinsfolk. It is of interest that in both phrases the term "except" is used, indicating that my reward is that and only that.

With a little reflection, we come to understand that following the path of Allah and the love of the Purified Household is one and the same, because if they were two, it would be a contradiction, that is, it cannot be said *I will only study in winter* and then say *I will only study in summer*. The restriction must be for the one thing only.

The Prophet ﷺ is ordered once to seek compensation from the people in the form of only following the path of Allah and in another instance, is ordered to seek compensation in the form of only love of kinship. In reality, these two requests are one. That is, the path of Allah is the love of the Purified Household.

From the point of view of love of the Purified Household^, two things are necessary: One is comprehension of and knowledge of the Purified Household, so who does not know them cannot possibly be passionate for them.   The second, is submissiveness and adherence, as love without obedience is a form of fakery, a sham, a form of lip service and a lie.   So, anyone who takes orders from any other than the Purified Household^ of the Prophetﷺ is yet to follow the path of Allah﷾. That is what the Holy Qur'ān is telling us.

As for the intellect, the rewards must be as heavy and weighty as the action. There is nothing as weighty or worthy of a reward for the message other than Imamate. The reward of the message is the continuation of the guidance it delivers, the reward of one Divinely Guided, is passing on the guidance to another Divinely Guided. The reward of the just, is passing on the work to another just person.

Our intellect tells us that where there is kindness there also needs to be gratitude, and if today the kindness of the Prophetﷺ has reached us and we have been guided to Islam, then we should compensate for it and if the reward for the guidance is the love of his kinship, today there must also be present his kinship for us to show love and obedience. Yes, today indeed we must show obedience and adherence to the Imam of our time, Imam Mahdi ﷺ. Otherwise, how could it be that we say Muslims, at the outset of Islam, were ordered to pay compensation for their guidance by being obedient to and showing love for the kinship of the Prophetﷺ, but in today's Islam, such a requirement is not present? Or that there is no kinship for us to be obedient and submissive to? Of course, the obedience and submissiveness to the Imam of our time, Imam Mahdi ﷺ, during the period of his occultation, is to work towards his message and go follow those he has entrusted, the scholars that are just and that have control over whims and desires.

Our intellect understands that, from the love of kinship as the reward for the Prophetﷺ that has led to hundreds of millions to guidance, happiness and great divine bounties, the kinship and those who fall under the banner requiring the love of kinship, are the best of the best and Divinely Guided. Therefore, the reward for the Divinely Guided Prophetﷺ can never be to love and follow one who has committed sin. It simply cannot be believed that people who have committed sin be loved and supported as compensation for all of time and obligated upon Muslims. No Islamic group (other than Shia

Islam) can identify their leader as Divinely Guided, sinless, and no one or group till now has ever narrated sin being committed by the Divinely Guided nor have they named a teacher for them.

Intellect tells placing guidance in the hand of a guide that is not Divinely Guided is not only oppressing humankind but oppression upon all of existence. That's because all of existence was created for mankind (all Ayāt indicate the existence was created for use by and the pleasure of mankind). So, is it not oppression upon mankind and all of existence that for mankind to reach spiritual and real perfection, and to reach a level of divinity, to be guided by one who is not himself Divinely Guided?

If narrations tell us that the foundation of religion is to know, support and be guided by the Divinely Guided:

بني الاسلام على خمس...الولاية[1]

And if Imam Ali divides people between those who will go to heaven and those who will end up in hell:

قسيم الجنة والنار[2]

And if prayers are not accepted where there is no acceptance of the Guidance by the Divinely Guided[3], and if the love of kinship is a good deed[4], and if their visitation and seeking their assistance has been advised, it is all because of the chemistry of the love for kinship.

Two great Sunni scholars, Zamkhshari and Fakhrirāzi, in their own exegesis have stated that the Prophet has stated:

- Whoever dies upon the love of the Purified Household of the Prophet Mohammad dies a martyr.
- Whoever dies upon the friendship of the Purified Household of the Prophet Mohammad dies repentant.
- Whoever dies upon the love of the Purified Household of the Prophet Mohammad dies with perfected faith.

---

[1] (Al Kafi) V2 P18

[2] (Bihar Al Anwar بحار الأنوار) V5 P186

[3] (Bihar Al Anwar بحار الأنوار) V27 P168

[4] (Bihar Al Anwar بحار الأنوار) V43 P362

- Whoever dies upon the love of the Purified Household of the Prophet Mohammadﷺ dies based upon the tradition of the way of the Prophetﷺ.

So, the question now is, can love of kinship without submissiveness also be considered for martyrdom, forgiveness and perfection?

Under those very exegeses in the explanation of this Ayah they state that the Prophetﷺ said:

الا و من مات على بغض آل محمد جاء يوم يقوم القيامة مكتوب بين عينيه آيس من رحمة الله﷽

Whoever dies with animosity and hatred towards the kinship of Prophet Mohammadﷺ will be raised on the day of resurrection with writing between his eyes: They are despaired and deprived from the Mercy of Allah﷽.

الا ومن مات على بغض آل محمد مات كافرا

Whoever dies with animosity and hatred towards the kinship of Prophet Mohammadﷺ dies an unbeliever.

الا ومن مات على بغض آل محمد لم يشم رائحة الجنة

Whoever dies with animosity and hatred towards the kinship of Prophet Mohammadﷺ will not smell the aroma of paradise.

Fakhrirāzi in his exegeses states that once the Ayah for the love of kinship was revealed, it was asked of the Prophetﷺ who is it that it has been obligated upon us to love? The Prophetﷺ replies Ali, Fātima and her sons, and then adds that the Prophetﷺ states

فاطمة؃ بضعة منّى يؤذيني ما يؤذيها

Fātima؃ is a part of me, whoever hurts her, hurts me, and whoever hurts the Prophetﷺ is punished with the curse of Allah﷽:

﴿إِنَّ ٱلَّذِينَ يُؤْذُونَ ٱللَّـهَ وَرَسُولَهُ لَعَنَهُمُ ٱللَّـهُ فِى ٱلدُّنْيَا وَٱلْءَاخِرَةِ وَأَعَدَّ لَهُمْ عَذَابًا مُّهِينًا﴾

Those who hurt God and His Messenger -- them God has cursed in the present world and the world to come, and has prepared for them a humbling chastisement.

(Al Ahzab 33:57).

In the narrations, we read that Imam Hasan﷽ under the Ayah

{وَمَن يَقْتَرِفْ حَسَنَةً نَّزِدْ لَهُ فِيهَا حُسْنًا}

...and whosoever gains a good deed, We shall give him increase of good in respect of it. (Ash Shura 42:23).

Stated that a good deed is the love of us, The Purified Household[1].

اقتراف الحسنة مودّتنا اهل البيت[1]

---

[1] Exegesis of Namouna and Safi

Lesson 20 Imamat and Wilayat

The Final Message from The Prophet☻

{يَـٰٓأَيُّهَا ٱلرَّسُولُ بَلِّغْ مَآ أُنزِلَ إِلَيْكَ مِن رَّبِّكَ

وَإِن لَّمْ تَفْعَلْ فَمَا بَلَّغْتَ رِسَالَتَهُۥ وَٱللَّهُ يَعْصِمُكَ مِنَ ٱلنَّاسِ

إِنَّ ٱللَّهَ لَا يَهْدِى ٱلْقَوْمَ ٱلْكَـٰفِرِينَ}

O Messenger, deliver that which has been sent down [with regards to the Wilayah of Imam Ali] to thee from thy Lord; for if thou dost not, thou wilt not have delivered His Message. God will protect thee from [the evilness of] men [and those who are unable to tolerate hearing this message]. God guides not the people of the unbelievers. (Al-Māida 5:67).

In all of the Holy Qur'ān this is the one and only place that the Prophet☻ has been threatened with regards to reservation in delivering the message, in that if he does not announce it, all of the 23 years of deliverance will be useless.

The Honourable Messenger☻ said to Imam Ali☻ that if I do not deliver the message relating to your guardianship all of my deeds will be erased.

In this Ayah, a few points come to light relating to this topic:

1. Surah Al Māida is of the last Surahs that was revealed to the Prophet☻.

2. In this Ayah, instead of saying Oh Prophet, the term Oh Messenger has been used, indicating the significance of the message.

3. In place of ابلغ the term بلغ has been used for the word "deliver", which is a means of signifying a decisive, formal and important message.

4. The Prophetﷺ is threatened with the loss of his entire life's work being nullified if he does not announce this single important message.

5. The Prophetﷺ is not afraid for his own life, as history shows that when he was fighting idol worshippers alone and in the battles with the disbelievers, he was never afraid of danger. (while there were showers of stone and his companions were being tortured…now why would he be afraid for his life towards the end of his life and amongst his own companions?).

6. The message of the Ayah is not related to monotheism, Prophethood or resurrection, as these fundamentals where already established at the outset of the revelation in Mecca and there is no need for all this advice at the end of his life.

7. The message of the Ayah is not related to prayers, fasting, pilgrimage, Islamic taxes or Jihad, as these were clarified over the span of 23 years of revelation and invitation to Islam, and the people also acted upon these deeds and there was no concern over them.

All exegetists of the Shia and some of the Sunni schools indicate this Ayah is proof of the guardianship of Imam Aliﷺ and that it was revealed on the 18th of Dhil Hijja in the tenth year of Hijra on the return trip from the Farewell Pilgrimage and is when the well-known narration was stated:

من كنتُ مولاه فعلیّ مولاه

Whomever I was guardian over, so Aliﷺ is their guardian.

It was when the choices that need to be made for salvation and its path was made clear. Imam Baqirﷺ stated:

بنى الاسلام على خمس: على الصلاة والزكاة والصوم والحج والولاية ولم يناد بشئ كما نودى بالولاية،

فأخذ الناس بأربع وتركوا هذه

Islam is based upon five foundations: Prayers, Islamic Tax, Fasting, Pilgrimage, and Guardianship (of the Purified Household﷽), so the people accepted four and left this (the fifth, being guardianship).

The Wilayah/Guardianship Is the Perfection and Completion of The Message

{ٱلْيَوْمَ يَئِسَ ٱلَّذِينَ كَفَرُوا مِن دِينِكُمْ فَلَا تَخْشَوْهُمْ وَٱخْشَوْنِ ٱلْيَوْمَ أَكْمَلْتُ لَكُمْ دِينَكُمْ وَأَتْمَمْتُ عَلَيْكُمْ نِعْمَتِى وَرَضِيتُ لَكُمُ ٱلْإِسْلَٰمَ دِينًا}

Today (the day of the appointment of the Guardianship to Imam Ali) the unbelievers have despaired of your religion; therefore, fear them not, but fear you Me. Today I have perfected your religion for you, and I have completed My blessing upon you, and I have approved Islam for your religion. (Al Māida 5:3).

According to both Shia and Sunni schools, this part of the Ayah, starting from "Today I have perfected…" was revealed after the appointment of Imam Ali﷽ as the guardian in Ghadir Khumm[1].

Without even looking at narrations that have been passed on, from an intellectual point of view this relationship can be confirmed as the Ayah discusses four features of the day:

1. The day the disbelievers despaired.
2. The day the religion was perfected.
3. The day that the blessings of Allah﷽ upon mankind was completed.
4. The day Islam was accepted and approved as a complete religion by Allah﷽, and no other days other than the Day of Appointment for the Prophetﷺ, migration, the liberation of Mecca, the victories of battles… and all the rest with all their value, none could add up to the four important features identified in this Ayah.

So, it is only this day in Ghadir Khumm that can have the four points combined in the one place:

- As for the despair of the disbelievers, it is because the allegations, war and ill intentions towards the life of the Prophetﷺ, would remain unsuccessful, having had his death as being their only hope. With the appointment of Imam Ali﷽, it became understood by all that the death of the Prophetﷺ no longer meant the annihilation of

---

[1] Ghadir Khumm is the name of the location in which these Ayāt were revealed.

his religion, because a personality such as Imam Ali would take the Prophets place as guardian of the Nation. Here it was that all the disbelievers became hopeless.

- As for the perfection of the religion, it is because of all the religious requirements concerning the laws and principles of the religion were stipulated, but a Guardian over the religion was not appointed, a provision of the religion would remain missing.

- As for the completion of blessings, it is because the most significant blessing the Holy Qur'ān points towards is the identification of the Guardian. The Prophet passing away and the Nation remaining without a Guardian would be an action that a shepherd would never do to his flock. How could it be that the Divine Blessing be completed without the appointment of a Guardian.

- As for the approval of Allah, it is for the reason that every time a law is completed and justly carried out, it becomes the reason for His satisfaction.

For these reasons (perfection of religion, completion of blessings, Divine Approval and despair of disbelievers), we have in narrations of the Purified Household^ that Eid of Ghadir is considered one of the most significant festivals.

Sometimes the effect of something depends on gathering all the requirements together, such as fasting, where breaking the fast even moments before the call to prayer will render the fast void. From this point, the term "complete" is used:

$$\{أَتِمُّوا ٱلصِّيَامَ إِلَى ٱللَّيْلِ\}$$

Then complete the Fast unto the night (Al Baqarah 2:187).

And sometimes, it is that every part of the whole can have its own effect, such as the recitation of the Holy Qur'ān, in that reciting the whole Book is its completion or reading any part of it has its own rewards.

Sometimes, some parts are such that if they were not there, a part would be missing, despite the rest of the parts being present. Look at the example of the pilot and driver where an aeroplane and car without them would mean they are useless. Wilayah and the True Guardianship are just like that, because mankind is connecting to Allah and without Guardianship, creations and blessings become troublesome and mankind will not reach Allah.

Who Is The Guardian?

{إِنَّمَا وَلِيُّكُمُ ٱللَّهُ وَرَسُولُهُ وَٱلَّذِينَ ءَامَنُوا ٱلَّذِينَ يُقِيمُونَ ٱلصَّلَوٰةَ وَيُؤْتُونَ ٱلزَّكَوٰةَ وَهُمْ رَٰكِعُونَ}

Your friend is only God, and His Messenger, and the believers who perform the prayer and pay the alms, and bow them down. (Al Māidah 5:55).

The reason for the revelation of this Ayah, in both Sunni and Shia schools, is that a poor man entered the Mosque of the Prophet and sought help from the people. No one paid him alms. Imam Ali, while in a state of prayer, and specifically in rukoo', gifted him his ring. In honouring this generosity, revealed this Ayah.

The Prophet in Ghadir Khum, in order to show the status of Imam Ali, recited this Ayah, and Imam Ali recited this Ayah multiple times to indicate the same.

It's true that the best form of introduction is one where the quality and characteristics of the individual is stated and the audience find the individual themselves through that introduction (The Ayah does not mention the name of Imam Ali but describes his qualities and actions).

The Guardianship of Islamic Jurist is in line with the Guardianship of the Divinely Guided. In Maqboola of Omar Bin Handhala[1], we read a narration that states Imam Sādiq said look at he who narrates our traditions, and looks at our rules of what is permitted and forbidden, and knows our laws, so accept his judgement as it is I that have placed him as a judge over you.

---

[1] مقبوله عمر بن حنظله

Lesson 21 The Imam of The Time

Allah's✹ Successor In The World

{وَعَدَ ٱللَّهُ ٱلَّذِينَ ءَامَنُوا مِنكُمْ وَعَمِلُوا ٱلصَّلِحَٰتِ لَيَسْتَخْلِفَنَّهُمْ فِى ٱلْأَرْضِ كَمَا ٱسْتَخْلَفَ ٱلَّذِينَ مِن قَبْلِهِمْ وَلَيُمَكِّنَنَّ لَهُمْ دِينَهُمُ ٱلَّذِى ٱرْتَضَىٰ لَهُمْ وَلَيُبَدِّلَنَّهُم مِّن بَعْدِ خَوْفِهِمْ أَمْنًا يَعْبُدُونَنِى لَا يُشْرِكُونَ بِى شَيْئًا وَمَن كَفَرَ بَعْدَ ذَٰلِكَ فَأُولَٰٓئِكَ هُمُ ٱلْفَٰسِقُونَ}

God has promised those of you who believe and do righteous deeds that He will surely make you successors in the land, even as He made those who were before them successors, and that He will surely establish their religion for them that He has approved and will give them in exchange, after their fear, security: 'They shall serve Me, not associating with Me anything.' Whoso disbelieves after that, those – they are the ungodly. (An Nūr 24:55).

In the narrations, there are many traditions where we read from the Divinely Guided the full extent of this Ayah is the day of governance of Imam Mahdi✹.

In the Holy Qur'ān, the ultimate government will be run by the righteous is stipulated multiple times. For example:

{لِيُظْهِرَهُ عَلَى الدِّينِ كُلِّهِ}

That He may uplift it above every religion (Al Tawba 9:33).

Meaning that Islam will succeed over all other religions. Elsewhere:

{أَنَّ ٱلْأَرْضَ يَرِثُهَا عِبَادِىَ ٱلصَّٰلِحُونَ}

The earth shall be the inheritance of My righteous servants. (Al Ambiyā 21:105).

And:

{وَٱلْعَٰقِبَةُ لِلْمُتَّقِينَ}

The issue ultimate is to the godfearing. (Al A'rāf 7:128, Al Qasas 28:83).

The meaning of "successors" in this Ayah is either that of the righteous successors from Allah﷽ or the ruin of the corrupt governments and replacing them with the righteous government.

"Qurtabi", in his exegesis, in regard to the complete success of Islam narrates a number of hadiths that say on Earth, not a single dwelling will remain where Islam has not entered that house.

The Prophetﷺ, on the return trip of his last Pilgrimage in Ghadir Khum, appointed Imam Ali؏ as his successor on the order of his Lord﷽, and the Ayah was revealed that states today Allah﷽ has chosen for you Islam as your religion (Holy Qur'ān 5:3). In the same Ayah Allah﷽ promises the victory of this religion which he has approved:

{دِينَهُمُ ٱلَّذِى ٱرْتَضَىٰ لَهُمْ}

Their religion for them that He has approved (An Nur 24:55).

And the religion the Allah﷽ has approved and announced is that very religion of Ghadir Khumm.

Messages that can be taken away from this Ayah are:

1. Islam is the future religion of the world. The future of history will be for the benefit of the believers and the demise of the dominating disbelievers. *"God has promised..., and that He will surely establish their religion".*

2. The disadvantaged believers are given hope so that they can withstand the pressures and hardships they are going through, and they do not despair as a result of them. *"God has promised those of you who believe"*.

3. The key and secret ingredient to obtaining rightful and widespread governance is only faith and good deeds. *"God has promised those of you who believe and do righteous deeds…"* is a promise who have faith and perform good deeds, not just who have faith.

4. Religion and politics are not separate, but rather, politics and government are there for the preservation of religion. *"make you successors in the land….'They shall serve Me"*.

5. In propagation and guiding the community, in order to make them believe, an example of history is indicated. *"Even as He made those who were before them successors"*.

6. The final victory will be to those who are with the Truth, one Divine Tradition. *"Even as He made those who were before them successors"*.

7. The goal for the victory of the people of Truth and faith is the settlement and stability of the Divine Religion on earth, and to arrive to monotheism and complete safety and security. *"He will surely establish their religion…and will give them in exchange….not associating with"*.

8. The religion of Islam is the only religion that will be to the Divine Contentment of Allah. *"Religion for them that He has approved"*.

9. True security and safety come under the shadow of a theocratic government. *"And will give them in exchange, after their fear, security."*

10. Under the pious government will be a group that will be deviated. *"God has promised…. Whoso disbelieves after that"*.

Remnant Of God بقية الله

In narrations, wherever there is a blessed presence of the Divine Will for something to be retained from humanity, is referred to as "Remnant of God", or بقية الله (Baqqiyat Allah), an example, are the believing soldiers that return triumphantly from the battlefield, and are so called, having survived with the will of Allah, Remnants of God.

In reference to the Imam of our Time, the term is also used, because by Divine Will, he has been held back for the guidance of mankind's remembrance and guarded away from the people.

In narrations, we have that one of his blessed names is Remnant of God and we refer to him by this name:

السلام علیک یا بقیة الله فی ارضه

Peace be upon you of Remnant of God on His land.

At the time of his reappearance, the Ayah 86 of Surah Hud will be recited

{بَقِيَّتُ ٱللَّهِ خَيْرٌ لَّكُمْ إِن كُنتُم مُّؤْمِنِينَ}

God's remainder is better for you, if you are believers. And I am not a guardian over you. (Hud 11:86).

And he will then say I am he who is the Remnant of God.

Of course, this title has also been given to the other Divinely Guided.

Lesson 22 Intercession

Intercession and Conditions of Intercession

{يَوْمَئِذٍ لَّا تَنفَعُ ٱلشَّفَٰعَةُ إِلَّا مَنْ أَذِنَ لَهُ ٱلرَّحْمَٰنُ وَرَضِىَ لَهُۥ قَوْلًا}

Upon that day the intercession will not profit (anyone), save for him to whom the
All-merciful gives leave, and whose speech (the one who seeks or gives the
intercession) He approves. (Tā Hā 20:109).

Denial of intercession is in contradiction of the Holy Qur'ān and narrations and is the source of despair for believers who commit sins, and acceptance of unconditional intercession or qualification is the reason for the defiance of wrongdoers and is contrary to Divine Justice, so the Holy Qur'ān has clarified for us that there is accounting and record keeping required for intercession.

In the Holy Qur'āns' point of view, intercession, gives a window of hope for those who sin and a vehicle for a relationship with the Divinely Chosen Guardians and to be able to follow them.

Intercession requires the permission from Allah and those who can enjoy it will only be those who pivot around monotheism, have the correct logic and fundamental beliefs of Truth, what they say is of the acceptance of Allah, that is, they proclaim the Two Witnesses (That there is No God but Allah and that the Muhammad is His Prophet) is not thematic, seasonal, coerced, shallow or based on mockery or hypocrisy. In that case, if their deeds come short of the necessary requirements then intercession can come in to play.

From this point of view, the Holy Qur'ān views as null and void the intercession of idols for the idol-worshippers in this world and in the hereafter.

Intercession does not mean that all the sins of the followers of Prophet Jesus are cleansed or that the Shia Muslims have their sins purified through the martyrdom of Imam Husain, although the Imam is one of the major intercessors on the Day of Judgement, however, it must be known that the aim of his martyrdom was not to intercede on behalf of his followers.

In relation to this Ayah, Imam Baqir stated that the intercession of the Prophet is only for those whose views and words were accepted, and lived for the love of the Purified Household, and dies for it:[1]

لَا يَنَالُ شَفَاعَةُ مُحَمَّدٍ ص يَوْمَ الْقِيَامَةِ إِلَّا مَنْ أَذِنَ لَهُ بِطَاعَةِ آلِ مُحَمَّدٍ وَ رَضِيَ لَهُ قَوْلًا وَ عَمَلًا فِيهِمْ فَحَيِيَ عَلَى مَوَدَّتِهِمْ وَ مَاتَ عَلَيْهَا

Intercessors and Those Who Receive Intercession

{وَكَم مِّن مَّلَكٍ فِي ٱلسَّمَٰوَٰتِ لَا تُغْنِي شَفَٰعَتُهُمْ شَيْئًا إِلَّا مِن بَعْدِ أَن يَأْذَنَ ٱللَّهُ لِمَن يَشَآءُ وَيَرْضَىٰ}

How many an angel there is in the heavens whose intercession avails not anything, save after that God gives leave to whomsoever He wills and is well-pleased. (An Najm 53:26).

{فَمَا تَنفَعُهُمْ شَفَٰعَةُ ٱلشَّٰفِعِينَ}

Then the intercession of the intercessors shall not profit them. (Al Muddathir 74:48).

In the Holy Qur'ān and in the narrations, we read that on the Day of Resurrection, certain individuals will be granted permission to intercede on behalf of others.

---

[1] (تأويل الآيات - Taw'eel Al Ayat)

The Prophetﷺ: In a narration from the Prophetﷺ we read that he stated *I am the first of intercessors.*[1]

انا اوّل شافع

The Holy Qur'ān: Imam Ali﷽ states that *the Qur'ān is an intercessor.*[2]

Prophets^: It has come in to narrations that Prophets provide intercession on the Day of Resurrection.[3]

یشفع الانبیاء

The Divinely Guided Guardians and the True Shias: A narration from a Divinely Guided Imam﷽ states that *In the Resurrection, intercession will be for us and our supporters.*[4]

لنا شفاعة و لاهل مودّتنا شفاعة

Angels and Martyrs: On the Day of Resurrection, permission has been given to angels and martyrs to intercede on behalf of whomever they wish.[5]

یؤذن للملائکة و الشهداء ان یشفعوا

On that Day, every martyr can intercede on behalf of seventy individuals from their family.[6]

Worship: From the reasons for intercession on the Day of Resurrection is the worship performed. *Fasting and the Qur'ān are intercessors to the worshipper on the Day of Resurrection."*[7]

الصيام والقرآن شفیعان للعبد يوم القيامة

---

[1] (Sahih Muslim) V2 P130

[2] (Nahjul Balagha) Speech 176

[3] (Musnad Ahmad) V3 P12

[4] (خصال Khisal) P624

[5] (Musnad Ahmad) V5 P43

[6] (سنن اب داود - Sunan Abu Dawood) V3 P15

[7] (Musnad Ahmad) V2 P174

Conditions For Receiving Intercession

The Holy Qur'ān and narrations point to conditions for those who will be able to enjoy intercession:

- People of faith, prayer, charity in the Cause of Allah⬥ and who do not waste away their life. *Then the intercession of the intercessors shall not profit them. (Al Muddathir 74:48).*
- Allah⬥ will give permission for the intercession to take place. *Who is there that shall intercede with Him save by His leave? (Holy Qur'ān 2:255).*
- Passes away with faith.
- There is a relationship between the intercessor and the one receiving intercession. One who does not have a faith inter-relationship with the intercessor will not be able to be a recipient of their intercession.

QUESTION: Is not intercession a form of "it's who you know or are related to"?

ANSWER: No. Because:

- One who receives intercession will make intercession possible by their own thoughts and deeds. So, contrary to "who you know or are related to", intercession is based upon laws and criteria.
- In intercession, no rights are forgone. Whereas in intervention through relationships, someone else's rights are abused.
- The intercessor does not have any expectations from the one seeking intercession. Where as in intervention through relations, there is an expectation of the recipient.
- The goal of the intercessor for the one receiving the intercession is for their redemption and salvation. Where as in intervention through relations, is a worldly success.
- Intercession is a form of nurturing and growth, because the recipient will have a spiritual relationship with those close to Allah⬥, the intercessors.

QUESTION: Will intercession not encourage people to sin?

ANSWER: Never, because firstly it is not known who will be granted intercession and secondly, will the formulation an anti-venom encourages people to get themselves poisoned and consume venom!?

Lesson 23 Sins and Disobedience

Kinds Of Sins

{ٱلَّذِينَ يَجْتَنِبُونَ كَبَٰئِرَ ٱلْإِثْمِ وَٱلْفَوَٰحِشَ إِلَّا ٱللَّمَمَ إِنَّ رَبَّكَ وَٰسِعُ ٱلْمَغْفِرَةِ}

Those who avoid the major sins and immoralities, only [committing] slight ones.

Indeed, your Lord is vast in forgiveness. (An Najm 53:32).

Every sin is referred as an immorality, such as adultery. For the term "slight ones", ٱللَّمَمَ, different meanings could be derived. Such as:

1. Sins that are heedless and not consistently committed.
2. Sins that have been decided upon, but not acted on.
3. Sins that have been committed but then forgiveness and repentance is sought for.
4. Sins that have no punishment promised for them.
5. Sins that have not had a punishment assigned to them.

Disobedience of Allah﷾, no matter how small, is significant, however by the same token, not all sins are equal. Some sins such as lying and back biting are considered more obscene and have higher severity in punishment assigned to them. Likewise, the time the sin is committed, the place the sin is committed, the intention of the sinner who committed the sin, their knowledge or ignorance with regards to the sin, insistence upon its commitment or otherwise, all have implications.

Imam Ali﷽ stated that the worst of sins is one that considered small or light.

اشد الذنوب ما استخف به صاحبه

Imam Riḍha﷽ indexes sins in the following manner:

Killing a soul, adultery, theft, consuming alcohol, dissatisfaction of and disownment of parents, running away from the battlefield, acting oppressively with the wealth of an orphan, consuming meat of a dead animal (not slaughtered in the Islamic manner), consuming blood and pig, and anything not slaughtered in the name of Allah﷽, taking usury, taking bribery, gambling, selling items with less weight than stated, throwing allegations at virtuous women, homosexuality, false testimonies, losing hope in the mercy of Allah﷽, considering oneself hell-bound with certainty, despair from the Divine Mercy, assisting and relying on oppressors, lying under oath, withholding the rights of others, lying, arrogance, squandering, wastefulness, treason, shortcomings in performing the pilgrimage (when one was able to), enmity towards the Divinely Guided Guardians^, being engaged in entertainment and play, and insistence upon sin.

Some factors and conditions will change "minor" sins in to "major" ones, such as:

Consistency in the committing of minor sins, considering the sin minor and light, feeling of joy or satisfaction while committing the sin, committing the sin out of rebellion, making one's sins apparent to others, sins of those who have a high status in society.

The Effects of And Consequences of Sin

Sin and disobedience have an effect on the soul and psychology of an individual, their family and society, place, time and the generations that follow will be greatly affected. For example, the Holy Qur'ān and narrations tell us that some of the effects of sin and disobedience are: The bringing of Divine Punishment (considering sin is contrary to intellect and natural instinct), hardening of the heart, the stripping of blessings, the rejection of supplication, the changing of provisions granted, being deprived of the ability to pray the Night Prayers, sudden calamities, lack of rain, the destruction of homes, disgrace, shortening of one's life, earthquakes, poverty, illness, being dominated by evil…. etc.

The Path to Restitution

1.   Repentance and compensation to make up for sins:

{إِلَّا مَن تَابَ وَءَامَنَ وَعَمِلَ صَلِحًا فَأُوْلَٰئِكَ يَدْخُلُونَ ٱلْجَنَّةَ وَلَا يُظْلَمُونَ شَيْئًا}

Save him who repents, and believes, and does a righteous deed; those -- they shall enter Paradise, and they shall not be wronged anything; (Maryam 19:60).

2.   Faith and good deeds:

{وَٱلَّذِينَ ءَامَنُوا وَعَمِلُوا ٱلصَّلِحَٰتِ لَنُكَفِّرَنَّ عَنْهُمْ سَيِّئَاتِهِمْ وَلَنَجْزِيَنَّهُمْ أَحْسَنَ ٱلَّذِى كَانُوا يَعْمَلُونَ}

And those who believe, and do righteous deeds, We shall surely acquit them of their evil deeds, and shall recompense them the best of what they were doing. (Al Ankabūt (29:7).

3.   Seeking forgiveness for one's own self and for others:

{فَٱسْتَغْفَرُوا ٱللَّهَ وَٱسْتَغْفَرَ لَهُمُ ٱلرَّسُولُ}

And prayed forgiveness of God, and the Messenger had prayed forgiveness for them (An Nisā 4:64).

4.   Prayers:

{وَأَقِمِ ٱلصَّلَوٰةَ ... إِنَّ ٱلْحَسَنَٰتِ يُذْهِبْنَ ٱلسَّيِّئَاتِ ذَٰلِكَ ذِكْرَىٰ لِلذَّٰكِرِينَ}

And perform the prayer... surely the good deeds will drive away the evil deeds. (Hud 11:114).

5.   Avoiding major sins:

{إِن تَجْتَنِبُوا كَبَآئِرَ مَا تُنْهَوْنَ عَنْهُ نُكَفِّرْ عَنكُمْ سَيِّئَاتِكُمْ وَنُدْخِلْكُم مُّدْخَلًا كَرِيمًا}

If you avoid the heinous sins that are forbidden you, We will acquit you of your evil deeds, and admit you by the gate of honour. (An Nisā 4:31).

6.   Joining struggles and martyrdom:

{وَقَٰتَلُوا۟ وَقُتِلُوا۟ لَأُكَفِّرَنَّ عَنْهُمْ سَيِّـَٔاتِهِمْ}

And fought, and were slain -- them I shall surely acquit of their evil deeds (Āle Imrān 3:195).

7. Paying alms and helping those in need:[1]

صدقة السر تكفر الخطيئة

Charity given in secrecy covers the mistakes.

8. Solving the problems of others:

من ۞فارات الذنوب العظام اغاثة الملهوف

From the atonement of the great sins are coming to the aid of the heart broken.

9-11. Greeting with a "Salam" (Peace be Upon you), giving food and Night Prayers:

ثلاث ۞فارات: افشاء السلام و اطعام الطعام و الصلاة بالليل و الناس نيام

Three atonements: The giving of greetings (Salam), the feeding of food, and the Prayers of the Night while people are asleep.

12. The recitation of praise upon Mohammadﷺ and his Purified Household:

فانها تهدم الذنوب ذنباً

For it destroys the sin of all sins.

Seeking Forgiveness

{رَبَّنَا ٱغْفِرْ لَنَا وَلِإِخْوَٰنِنَا ٱلَّذِينَ سَبَقُونَا بِٱلْإِيمَٰنِ}

Our Lord, forgive us and our brothers, who preceded us in belief. (Al Hashr 59:10).

Forgiveness is the coming out of the pit, while repentance is the movement.

---

[1] Translators note: See also Holy Qur'ān 2:271

Forgiveness is the cleansing of the sin; repentance is to return to a pure heart.

The Prophetﷺ was himself amongst those who sought forgiveness as well as one who advised *Seek forgiveness from your Nurturer and then repent to him.*

استغفروا ربكم ثم توبوا اليه

We should not only seek forgiveness for ourselves but should also ask the Divine Guardians to seek intercession on our behalf.

{يَٰٓأَبَانَا ٱسْتَغْفِرْ لَنَا ذُنُوبَنَآ}

Our father, ask forgiveness for us (Yusuf 12:97).

The Prophetﷺ stated that my life and death for you is to your benefit. In my life, Allahﷻ takes punishment away from reaching you and after my death, with your deeds being presented to me, with your requests of forgiveness and pardon through me, will also be to your benefit.

{وَلَوْ أَنَّهُمْ إِذ ظَّلَمُوٓا أَنفُسَهُمْ جَآءُوكَ فَٱسْتَغْفَرُوا ٱللَّهَ
وَٱسْتَغْفَرَ لَهُمُ ٱلرَّسُولُ لَوَجَدُوا ٱللَّهَ تَوَّابًا رَّحِيمًا}

If, when they wronged themselves, they had come to thee, and prayed forgiveness of God, and the Messenger had prayed forgiveness for them, they would have found God turns, All-compassionate. (An Nisā 4:64).

Just as seeking forgiveness through the Prophetﷺ is of benefit (Ayah 4:64 above), so is seeking it through the pious and the angels. In the Holy Qur'ān, each of these has been proposed.

{وَٱلْمَلَٰٓئِكَةُ يُسَبِّحُونَ بِحَمْدِ رَبِّهِمْ وَيَسْتَغْفِرُونَ لِمَن فِى ٱلْأَرْضِ}

And when the angels proclaim the praise of their Lord, and ask forgiveness for those on earth. (Ash Shura 42:5).

{وَيَسْتَغْفِرُونَ لِلَّذِينَ ءَامَنُوا}

And they ask forgiveness for those who believe (Ghafir 40:7).

The visitation of the Divine Guards and appealing and begging through them, is supported through the Holy Qur'ān.

Of course, the Prophetﷺ is not who forgives the sins, but is rather an intermediary to Divine Forgiveness. Therefore, for those who have erred, they must at first be regretful and return to the path of truth, thereafter for the strengthening of their relationship with Allah؊, request help from the Prophetic Mission.

{وَمَا كَانَ ٱللَّهُ لِيُعَذِّبَهُمْ وَأَنتَ فِيهِمْ

وَمَا كَانَ ٱللَّهُ مُعَذِّبَهُمْ وَهُمْ يَسْتَغْفِرُونَ}

But God would never chastise them, with thee among them; God would never

chastise them as they begged forgiveness. (Al Anfāl 8:33).

The above Ayah indicates the reservation of the unleashing of the wrath of Allah؊ upon the Muslims by the grace of the presence of the Prophetﷺ amongst them, just as in the delaying of punishments of previous nations, despite there being certain people deserving of Divine Punishment.

Disobedience and committing of some sins are the cause of the deliverance of Divine Punishment and the way towards restitution is repentance and seeking forgiveness.

{وَمَا كَانَ ٱللَّهُ مُعَذِّبَهُمْ وَهُمْ يَسْتَغْفِرُونَ}

God would never chastise them as they begged forgiveness. (Al Anfāl 8:33)

And

{وَمَا كَانَ رَبُّكَ لِيُهْلِكَ ٱلْقُرَىٰ بِظُلْمٍ وَأَهْلُهَا مُصْلِحُونَ}

Yet thy Lord would never destroy the cities unjustly, while as yet their people were

putting things right. (Hud 11:117).

We also have in the narrations that until such time that amongst the people are virtuous and pious individuals, Allah؊ would withhold punishment and the delivery of hardship to the others. Such as the eradication of the Nation of Lot؊, where Prophet Abraham؊ asked the angels to deliver their punishment, that amongst them is Prophet Lot؊, meaning would they deliver the punishment while he was amongst them? The angels replied that they are aware of his presence and have ordered him to leave that area.

Or such as Imam Ali﷽ after the passing of the Prophet﷽, stated that one of two of your security has passed, so keep the second, which is forgiveness, well protected.

Or Imam Riḍha﷽ when he said to Zakaria son of Adam, that you should remain in Qom so that just as the Divine Punishment did not fall upon the people of Baghdad for the sake of Imam Kadhim﷽, based upon your presence, calamities upon that city will be distanced.

Seeking forgiveness pushes away calamities. Repentance and seeking forgiveness has significance and value with Allah﷽, so much so that the final destination of a nation may be rewritten - *God would never chastise them as they begged forgiveness.*

Sinners must not despair; seeking forgiveness, repentance and visitations of Divine Guardians is a route to spiritual return and upliftment. Of course, seeking forgiveness for disbelievers and hypocrites has no value or effect.

{سَوَآءٌ عَلَيْهِمْ أَسْتَغْفَرْتَ لَهُمْ أَمْ لَمْ تَسْتَغْفِرْ لَهُمْ}

Equal it is for them, whether thou askest forgiveness for them or thou askest not

forgiveness for them. (Al Munafiqūn 63:6).

Lesson 24 Repentance
The Features of Repentance in The Holy Qur'ān

{إِلَّا مَن تَابَ وَآمَنَ وَعَمِلَ صَالِحًا فَأُولَـٰئِكَ يَدْخُلُونَ الْجَنَّةَ وَلَا يُظْلَمُونَ شَيْئًا}

Save him who repents, and believes, and does a righteous deed; those -- they shall

enter Paradise, and they shall not be wronged anything (Maryam 19:60).

Generally, the Holy Qur'ān follows Ayāt regarding punishment with words such as "Save him who repents" or "Except those who repent", indicating that: the path to reconciliation is never closed to anyone.

1.   Repentance is an obligation upon us; because Allahﷻ states that we should collectively seek repentance to Allahﷻ:

{وَتُوبُوا إِلَى اللَّـهِ}

And turn all together to God (An Nur 24:31).

2.   The acceptance of the authentic and genuine repentance is a certainty, it is impossible for us to obey His command to seek repentance but for Him to reject it.

{وَهُوَ الَّذِى يَقْبَلُ التَّوْبَةَ عَنْ عِبَادِهِ}

It is He who accepts repentance from His servants (Ash Shu'ara 42:25).

{هُوَ التَّوَّابُ الرَّحِيمُ}

He is All-forgiving and All-merciful. (Al Baqarah 2:37).

3. Allah❀ not only accepts true repentance but also loves those who repent much.

{إِنَّ اللَّـهَ يُحِبُّ التَّوَّابِينَ}

Truly, God loves those who repent (constantly).(Al Baqarah 2:222).

Repentance must be accompanied by pure action and sins be resituated

{ثُمَّ تَابَ مِن بَعْدِهِ وَأَصْلَحَ}

And thereafter repents and makes amends. (Al Anām 6:54).

4. Repentance Is the secret to redemption.

{... وَتُوبُوا إِلَى اللَّـهِ... لَعَلَّكُمْ تُفْلِحُونَ}

And turn all together to God... haply so you will prosper. (An Nūr 24:31).

5. Repentance is the means to which sinful deeds are transformed into good deeds.

{إِلَّا مَن تَابَ وَآمَنَ وَعَمِلَ عَمَلًا صَالِحًا فَأُولَـٰئِكَ يُبَدِّلُ اللَّـهُ سَيِّئَاتِهِمْ حَسَنَاتٍ}

Save him who repents, and believes, and does righteous work -- those, God will

change their evil deeds into good deeds. (Al Furqān 25:70).

6. Repentance is the cause for rain to come down and for blessings from the skies

{تُوبُوا إِلَيْهِ يُرْسِلِ السَّمَاءَ}

And, O my people! As forgiveness of your Lord, then turn to Him; He will send on

you clouds pouring down abundance of rain. (Hūd 11:52).

7. Repentance is the cause of pure sustenance.

{تُوبُوا إِلَيْهِ يُمَتِّعْكُم مَّتَاعًا حَسَنًا}

Repent to Him, and He will give you fair enjoyment.

(Hūd 11:13).

8. Repentance committed when the effects of death are upon us or during times of punishment is not accepted.

{حَتَّىٰ إِذَا حَضَرَ أَحَدَهُمُ الْمَوْتُ قَالَ إِنِّى تُبْتُ الْآنَ}

When one of them is visited by death, he says, 'Indeed now I repent,' (An Nisā 4:18).

9. Allah, accepts repentance, as well as showing Mercy upon his servants. Alongside Ayāt of repentance the attributes of Mercy, Gentleness and Compassion are indicated.

{هُوَ التَّوَّابُ الرَّحِيمُ}

He is All-forgiving and All-merciful. (Al Baqarah 2:37).

{ثُمَّ تَابَ عَلَيْهِمْ إِنَّهُ بِهِمْ رَءُوفٌ رَّحِيمٌ}

then He turned towards them; surely He is Gentle to them, and All-compassionate. (Al Tawba 9:117).

{ثُمَّ تَابَ عَلَيْهِمْ إِنَّهُ بِهِمْ رَءُوفٌ رَّحِيمٌ}

God forgave them because of His Compassion and Mercy. (Al Tawba 9:117).

{ثُمَّ تُوبُوا إِلَيْهِ إِنَّ رَبِّي رَحِيمٌ وَدُودٌ}

And turn to Him in repentance. My Lord is certainly All-merciful and Loving. (Hūd 11:90).

10. The Holy Qur'ān views the abandonment of repentance as oppression and self-annihilation

{وَمَن لَّمْ يَتُبْ فَأُولَٰئِكَ هُمُ الظَّالِمُونَ}

And whoso repents not, those -- they are the evildoers (Al Hujurāt 49:11).

{ثُمَّ لَمْ يَتُوبُوا فَلَهُمْ عَذَابُ جَهَنَّمَ}

and then have not repented, there awaits them the chastisement of Hell (Burūj 85:10).

Conditions of The Acceptance of Repentance

Ayah 17 of Surah An Nisā gives us one aspect of the conditions of acceptance of Repentance:

{إِنَّمَا التَّوْبَةُ عَلَى اللَّـهِ لِلَّذِينَ يَعْمَلُونَ السُّوءَ بِجَهَالَةٍ ثُمَّ يَتُوبُونَ مِن قَرِيبٍ فَأُولَـٰئِكَ يَتُوبُ اللَّـهُ عَلَيْهِمْ ۗ وَكَانَ اللَّـهُ عَلِيمًا حَكِيمًا}

God shall turn only towards those who do evil in ignorance, then shortly repent;
God will return towards those; God is All-knowing, All-wise. (An Nisā 4:17)

A) The sins for which repentance are accepted are those committed out of ignorance unintentionally, not those committed out of stubbornness and disobedience.
B) Repent quickly, before the sin besieges the sinner, or it becomes a characteristic of the individual, or the wrath and divine punishment be sent down.

Imam Sādiq states: Every sin that one commits, even if committed while aware, is in fact committed ignorantly, for they have put themselves in the path of Divine Wrath.

Of course, one who committed sin and repents is similar to one who has not committed sin and like a new born child that has just been born, pure, pure.

Repentance Is Lifesaving

{فَلَوْلَا كَانَتْ قَرْيَةٌ آمَنَتْ فَنَفَعَهَا إِيمَانُهَا إِلَّا قَوْمَ يُونُسَ لَمَّا آمَنُوا كَشَفْنَا عَنْهُمْ عَذَابَ الْخِزْيِ فِي الْحَيَاةِ الدُّنْيَا وَمَتَّعْنَاهُمْ إِلَىٰ حِينٍ}

Why was there never a city that believed, and its belief profited it? -- Except the
people of Jonah; when they believed, We removed from them the chastisement of
degradation in this present life, and We gave unto them enjoyment for a time.
(Yunus 10:98).

In the exegesis, we see that Prophet Yunus preached worship to his people for many years, but amongst the many people he preached to, only two people believed as a result, one who was a worshipper and the other a wise scholar. Prophet Yunus ﷺ, by the suggestion of the worshipper, took to cursing the people and left them behind. Little did he know that this will be the cause of difficulties sent his way from Allah.

Prophet Yunus ﷺ boarded a ship destined to another place. During the voyage, a large whale rammed the boat and it was not going to be long before everyone on board would drown at sea. The people on board decided to throw a man overboard so that the rest can escape the whale. In order to choose who to sacrifice, they decided to draw lots, in which Prophet Yunus' ﷺ was picked, and subsequently was thrown overboard. The whale swallowed him up without hesitation, but by Divine order, was not chewed or digested.

Prophet Yunus ﷺ, in the darkness with in the whale and in the depths of the waters, acknowledged the oppression he committed upon himself, the misplaced curse he sent upon the people and his departure from them. Allah﷽ accepted his supplication and granted him salvation from the situation he was in. Since then, Prophet Yunus ﷺ was given the name "ذو النون " (Dhul Al Noon), a name given to him as a result of this incident, and which is mentioned in the Ayāt of 87 and 88 of Surah Al Ambiyāa (21:87-88).

Sometime later, he returned to the people he left behind and found that they had not been destroyed. Upon inquiry, it was explained to him that the wise scholar, upon witnessing the curse and the signs of punishment coming down, rose and called to the people to be warned and cautioned. The people were affected and were guided by the wise scholar to leave their city and separate themselves from their children, they cried and supplicated to their Lord, and their Lord accepted their repentance and saved them from their certain punishment.

Yes, man can not only avert certain punishment and torment with faith, repentance and invocation, even when overbalancing on the cusp of the proverbial cliff, but also reach success.

The story of the repentance of the people of Prophet Yunus ﷺ was in the middle of the Ayah and was hinted at, but the Surah was named Surah Yunus ﷺ, perhaps because of the sensitivity and importance of the actions of the people of Yunus, that at the last moment they repented, and their repentance was accepted.

Lesson 25 The Return

Audit of The Day of Resurrection

{اقْتَرَبَ لِلنَّاسِ حِسَابُهُمْ وَهُمْ فِي غَفْلَةٍ مُّعْرِضُونَ}

Nigh unto men has drawn their reckoning, while they in heedlessness are yet turning away; (Al Ambiyā 21:1).

From what we find from the Ayāt of the Holy Qur'ān:

1. Every individual will be subjected to interrogation:

{فَلَنَسْأَلَنَّ الَّذِينَ أُرْسِلَ إِلَيْهِمْ وَلَنَسْأَلَنَّ الْمُرْسَلِينَ}

So We shall question those unto whom a Message was sent, and We shall question the Envoys. (Al Aarāf 7:6).

2. All of our deeds will be accounted for

{وَلَتُسْأَلُنَّ عَمَّا كُنتُمْ تَعْمَلُونَ}

And you will surely be questioned about the things you wrought. (An Nahl 16:93).

3. All matters under all circumstances will be under investigation

{وَإِن تُبْدُوا مَا فِي أَنفُسِكُمْ أَوْ

{تُخْفُوهُ يُحَاسِبْكُم بِهِ اللَّـهُ}

Whether you publish what is in your hearts or hide it, God shall make reckoning with you for it. (Al Baqara 2:284).

4. Questions will be asked of every part of our body

{إِنَّ السَّمْعَ وَالْبَصَرَ وَالْفُؤَادَ كُلُّ أُولَـٰئِكَ كَانَ عَنْهُ مَسْئُولًا}

The hearing, the sight, the heart -- all of those shall be questioned of. (Al Isrā 17:36).

5. Questions will be asked from the divine blessings one is blessed with

{ثُمَّ لَتُسْأَلُنَّ يَوْمَئِذٍ عَنِ النَّعِيمِ}

Then you shall be questioned that day concerning true bliss. (At Takāthur 102:8).

6. All actions conducted at any place no matter how little or significant

{إِن تَكُ مِثْقَالَ حَبَّةٍ مِّنْ خَرْدَلٍ فَتَكُن فِي صَخْرَةٍ أَوْ فِي السَّمَاوَاتِ أَوْ فِي الْأَرْضِ يَأْتِ بِهَا اللَّـهُ}

If it should be but the weight of one grain of mustard-seed, and though it be in a rock, or in the heavens, or in the earth, God shall bring it forth. (Luqmān 31:16).

The first question will be that of prayer and of items of such significance; youth, your life, how you earned a living and related expenses, how wealth was spent, and issues of who your leader and guide is will be asked, and all of this will be accounted for by Allah Himself

{وَكَفَىٰ بِنَا حَاسِبِينَ}

And sufficient are We for reckoners. (Al Ambiyā 21:47).

Different Ways of Being Accountable

On Resurrection Day, there will be different ways that people will be investigated:

1. A group that will have an easy interview and accounting

{حِسَابًا يَسِيرًا}

Receive an easy reckoning (Inshiqāq 84:8).

2.   Another group will be interrogated harshly and in detail

{حِسَابًا شَدِيدًا}

And then We made with it a terrible reckoning (Al Talāq 65:8).

3.   Some will be thrown straight in to hell without the need for any questioning or weighing up their deeds

{فَلَا نُقِيمُ لَهُمْ يَوْمَ الْقِيَامَةِ وَزْنًا}

And on the Day of Resurrection We shall not assign to them any weight. (Al Kahf 18: 105).

4.   While another will be granted paradise without question

{إِنَّمَا يُوَفَّى الصَّابِرُونَ أَجْرَهُم بِغَيْرِ حِسَابٍ}

Surely the patient will be paid their wages in full without reckoning. (Az Zumar 39:10).

According to many Ayāt, one who engages others with forgiveness and compassion will have an easy accounting, while those who engage others with difficulty and with detailed auditing will themselves be subjected to the same harshness. A disbelieving polytheist will go to hell without question, while people of patience will be granted paradise without question.[1]

Scroll Of Deeds

{وَكُلَّ إِنسَانٍ أَلْزَمْنَاهُ طَائِرَهُ فِي عُنُقِهِ
وَنُخْرِجُ لَهُ يَوْمَ الْقِيَامَةِ كِتَابًا يَلْقَاهُ مَنشُورًا}

And every man -- We have fastened to him his bird of omen upon his neck; and We shall bring forth for him, on the Day of Resurrection, a book he shall find spread wide open. (Al Isrā 17:14).

---

[1] Please refer to books on the topic of resurrection.

Multiple times in the Holy Qur'ān the issue of Scroll, or Book, of Deeds, and in different Ayāt, several issues are raised including:

1. A Scroll of Deeds is for everyone. (Al Isrā 17:13)
2. All deeds are in the Scroll. (Al Kahf 18:49)
3. Criminals will be in fear of it. (Al Kahf 18:49)
4. Everyone will be their own judge, upon reading their own Scroll. (Al Isra 17:14)
5. The pious will have their scroll handed to their right hand while hell dwellers will be to their left. (Al Haqqa 69:19,25)

Witnesses of The Court of Resurrection Day

As for witnesses, there are plenty:

1. Allah, a Witness overall and everything.

$$\{ \text{إِنَّ اللَّـهَ كَانَ عَلَىٰ كُلِّ شَىْءٍ شَهِيدًا} \}$$

God is witness over everything. (An Nisā 4:33)

2. The Prophet.

$$\{ \text{فَكَيْفَ إِذَا جِئْنَا مِن كُلِّ أُمَّةٍ بِشَهِيدٍ وَجِئْنَا بِكَ عَلَىٰ هَـٰؤُلَاءِ شَهِيدًا} \}$$

How then shall it be, when We bring forward from every nation a witness, and bring thee to witness against those? (An Nisā 4:41).

3. The Divinely Guided.

$$\{ \text{وَكَذَٰلِكَ جَعَلْنَاكُمْ أُمَّةً وَسَطًا}$$
$$\text{لِّتَكُونُوا شُهَدَاءَ عَلَى النَّاسِ} \}$$

Thus We appointed you a midmost nation that you might be witnesses to the people (Al Baqara 2:183).

According to the narrations, the nation in this Ayah refers to the Divinely Guided, as any other individual will not have the required knowledge or infallibility to be able to act as a witness on such a day.

4. Angels.

{وَجَاءَتْ كُلُّ نَفْسٍ مَّعَهَا سَائِقٌ وَشَهِيدٌ}

And every soul shall come, and with it a driver and a witness. (Qāf 50:21)

On judgement day, each person will be escorted by two angels, one as the driver, the other as the witness.

5.   The Earth.

{يَوْمَئِذٍ تُحَدِّثُ أَخْبَارَهَا}

Upon that day she shall tell her tidings (Zilzāl 99:4)

6.   Conscience.

{اقْرَأْ كِتَابَكَ كَفَىٰ بِنَفْسِكَ الْيَوْمَ عَلَيْكَ حَسِيبًا}

'Read thy book! Thy soul suffices thee this day as a reckoner against thee.' (Al Isrā 17:14).

7.   Parts of the body.

{يَوْمَ تَشْهَدُ عَلَيْهِمْ أَلْسِنَتُهُمْ وَأَيْدِيهِمْ وَأَرْجُلُهُم بِمَا كَانُوا يَعْمَلُونَ}

On the day when their tongues, their hands and their feet shall testify against them touching that they were doing. (An Nūr 24:24).

8.   Time.
Imam Sajjād ؏ in his sixth supplication of Sahifah Sajjādiya states:

هذا يوم حادث جديد وهو علينا شاهد عتيد

Today is a new fresh day, and it will bear witness upon us on the Day of Resurrection.

9.   Deeds.

{وَوَجَدُوا مَا عَمِلُوا حَاضِرًا}

And they shall find all they wrought present. (Al Kahf 18:49).

All deeds will be presented on the Day of Resurrection in their bodily reality and framed upon the doer of the deeds.

Forgive Until Forgiven

For the granting of the mercy of Allah, a method is provided to us in the Holy Qur'ān:

{وَلْيَعْفُوا وَلْيَصْفَحُوا أَلَا تُحِبُّونَ أَن يَغْفِرَ اللَّهُ لَكُمْ وَاللَّهُ غَفُورٌ رَّحِيمٌ}

But let them pardon and forgive. Do you not wish that God should forgive you?
God is All-forgiving, All-compassionate. (An Nūr 24:22)

If one truly seeks forgiveness from Allah, then one must also forgive others.

The Day of Resurrection is a day of accounting, punishment and reward, a lonesome day, and we must be thinking of our selves right now. The way to receiving the kindness of Allah on the Day is to be kind to others today, show beneficence and beneficence will be shown to you. Oh! so many were with us last months of Ramadhān that are not with us today, and this year may well be the last month of Ramadhān we have.

Lesson 26 Expenditure

Kinds Of Expenditure

{يَسْأَلُونَكَ مَاذَا يُنفِقُونَ قُلْ مَا أَنفَقْتُم مِّنْ خَيْرٍ فَلِلْوَالِدَيْنِ وَالْأَقْرَبِينَ وَالْيَتَامَىٰ وَالْمَسَاكِينِ وَابْنِ السَّبِيلِ وَمَا تَفْعَلُوا مِنْ خَيْرٍ فَإِنَّ اللَّـهَ بِهِ عَلِيمٌ}

They will question thee concerning what they should expend. Say: 'Whatsoever good you expend is for parents and kinsmen, orphans, the needy, and the traveller; and whatever good you may do, God has knowledge of it.'

(Al Baqara 2:215).

Expenditure is of five types:

1. Obligatory expenditure: Such as Khums, Zakāt, Kaffara, sacrificial and livelihood to our parents, children and partners (upon the husband).
2. Recommended expenditure: Helping the needy, orphans, and gifts to friends.
3. Banned expenditure: Such as spending money that has been unlawfully obtained or in the way of sin.
4. Disliked expenditure: Such as spending for others while there is needy kinsfolk.

5. General (other) expenditure: Spending for others to improve lifestyle, as opposed to help lift poverty which is mandatory or recommended.

The Best Kind of Expenditure

{لَن تَنَالُوا ٱلْبِرَّ حَتَّىٰ تُنفِقُوا مِمَّا تُحِبُّونَ}

You will not attain piety until you expend of what you love; (Āle Imrān 3:92)

The term "Al-Birr" in the above Ayah (translated as piety above), refers to goodness and blessings, and used in a place where there is farming and/or life develops. And with attention to the linguistic derivation of the word referring to the expansion of goodness, in the Holy Qur'ān, faith, pious deeds, Jihad, prayers and keeping one's word are samples of piety (or *Al-Birr*).

It has been recommended that in the process of piety one should accompany and assist each other.

{وَتَعَاوَنُوا عَلَى ٱلْبِرِّ}

Help one another to piety (Al Māida 5:2)

And the road to this priceless gem is in the above Ayah (3:92).

A Sample of The Expenditure of The Believers

1. Abu Talha Ansari, who had the greatest number of date palm trees in the Holy City of Medina and beautiful, prestige garden which produced a handsome income. This garden was opposite the Mosque of the Prophet☀, and had a water spring with crystal clear waters flowing from it. The Prophet ☀ would from time to time enter this garden to drink from the spring. When this Ayah "You will not attain piety until you expend of what you love" was revealed, Abu Talha Ansari came to the Prophet and said that the most beloved to me is this garden, and I want to give it in the way of Allah☀. The Prophet ☀ said that this is a good trade, and offered his praise, but suggested to offer this garden to the needy of his family and relatives. He accepted, and the garden was divided among them.

2. On the wedding night of Sayyida Fātima Al Zahra ☀, a poor person requested of her some old clothes. Sayyida Fātima ☀, with this Ayah in mind, changed out of her wedding garments and bestowed that to her.

3. Some guests entered upon Abu Dhar, and Abu Dhar said since he was pre-occupied, to slaughter a camel and prepare the meal. The guests choose a slim camel. Abu Dhar became somewhat uneasy and asked why they choose such skinny camel, to which the guests replied they left the other ones for a day when you would need them. Abu Dhar replied: The day I am in need is the day I am in my grave.

The Hand of The Needy is The Hand of Allah

Imam Sādiq stated that the alms does not reach the hand of the needy unless it goes through the Hand of Allah first. Then he recited this Ayah:

$$\{ أَلَمْ يَعْلَمُوٓا۟ أَنَّ ٱللَّـهَ هُوَ يَقْبَلُ ٱلتَّوْبَةَ عَنْ عِبَادِهِۦ وَيَأْخُذُ ٱلصَّدَقَـٰتِ \}$$

Do they not know that God is He who accepts repentance from His servants, and takes the freewill offerings, and that God. (Al Tawba 9:104).

Now that the receiver of the alms is Allah, so we should not only be giving to the needy with the warmest of heart, but be giving the best quality and in the best possible way.

When giving wealth in the way of Allah has the ability to ability to grow in to 700 times over and more, then what of the giving of life and soul in the way of Allah?

Martyrdom the Giving of the Soul

$$\{ وَلَا تَحْسَبَنَّ ٱلَّذِينَ قُتِلُوا۟ فِى سَبِيلِ ٱللَّهِ أَمْوَٰتًۢا بَلْ أَحْيَآءٌ عِندَ رَبِّهِمْ يُرْزَقُونَ \}$$

Count not those who were slain in God's way as dead, but rather living with their Lord, by Him provided. (Āle Imrān 3:169).

On the basis that we count those who are martyred as alive, we speak with them, send our peace and blessings to them and seek their intercession, especially the martyrs of Karbala. And now, some points about martyrdom are due to be clarified:

1. It has been narrated that there are seven attributes that are Divinely gifted to martyrs: The first drop of blood grants complete forgiveness of all sins, their heads rest on the laps of fair women with large

beautiful eyes, will be adorned in heavenly clothes, perfumed with the most sensual perfumes, will be able to see their place in heaven, they are allowed to wander through the entire heaven, curtains will be moved so they can seek to see God's Majesty.

2. In narrations, it is stated for every good there is better, except for martyrdom for which anything better cannot be imagined.

3. On the day of resurrection, a martyr will have the honourable position of intercessor.

4. They will enter through specially designated doors, enter Paradise before everyone else and have a designated area in Heaven.

5. Imam Ali ﷺ, having multiple special attributes, only at the moment of being struck and meeting his martyrdom, said "I swear by the Lord of The Kaaba I have become victorious". He was the first to embrace Islam, to sleep in the place of the Prophet ﷺ (to protect him from a plot to kill him while asleep), became the brother of the Prophet ﷺ, had the only door access direct to the Prophets Mosque in Medina from his home (while all others were ordered closed), is the father of the Imams and husband of Sayyida Fātima Al Zahra ﷺ (Divinely Guided daughter of the Prophet ﷺ). He destroyed idols, and his striking of the sword in Battle of Khandaq was better than the worship by the Jinn and mankind combined, but he did not say "I have become victorious" in any of these cases.

6. Imam Ali ﷺ swore by his Lord that the soul of the son of Abu Tālib is in his own hands, tolerating a thousand strikes by a sword for the sake of Allah ﷻ is easier than death while asleep in bed.

The Best Deed

{خَلَقَ السَّمَاوَاتِ وَالْأَرْضَ بِالْحَقِّ وَصَوَّرَكُمْ فَأَحْسَنَ صُوَرَكُمْ وَإِلَيْهِ الْمَصِيرُ}

He created the heavens and the earth with the truth, and He shaped you, and shaped you well; and unto Him is the homecoming. (Taghabun 64:3)

All of Allah's Deeds are the best deeds:

1. His creation is the best creation.[1]
2. His book, the Holy Qur'ān, is the best book.[2]

---

[1] Al Muiminūn 23:14
[2] Az Zumar 39:23

3. His stories are the best stories.[1]
4. His names are the best names.[2]
5. His rewards are the best rewards.[3]
6. His promises are the best there is.[4]
7. His judgement is the best of judgements.[5]

Allah۔ also wants of us to act upon the best of deeds, for example:

1. In our speech, say nothing but the best.[6]
2. In our deeds, do the very best of.[7]
3. In our altercations, have the best of manners.[8]
4. In discussions and debates, choose the best of methods.[9]
5. In gratitude and thankfulness, have the best of ways.[10]
6. Choose to listen to the very best of sayings.[11]
7. In monitoring the money of the orphaned, using the very best of methodologies.[12]
8. Our motivations, to have the purest of intentions and desires towards Allah۔, so that our deeds are tainted with the colour of Allah۔.[13]

---

[1] Yusuf 12:3
[2] Al Arāf 7:180
[3] Al Kahf 18:88
[4] An Nisā 4:95
[5] Māida 5:50
[6] Al Isra 17:53
[7] Al Kahf 18:7
[8] Al Muiminūn 23:96
[9] Al Nahl 16:125
[10] An Nisā 4:86
[11] Az Zumar 39:18
[12] Al Isra 17:34
[13] Al Anām 6:125

Lesson 27 The Mosque

The Importance of The Mosque

{وَأَنَّ الْمَسَاجِدَ لِلَّـهِ فَلَا تَدْعُوا مَعَ اللَّـهِ أَحَدًا}

The places of worship belong to God; so call not, along with God, upon anyone. (Al Jinn 72:18)

1. The first building ever on the face of the planet was a place of worship:

{إِنَّ أَوَّلَ بَيْتٍ وُضِعَ لِلنَّاسِ لَلَّذِى بِبَكَّةَ مُبَارَكًا وَهُدًى لِّلْعَالَمِينَ}

The first House established for the people was that at Bakka, a place holy, and a guidance to all beings. (Āle Imrān 3:96)

2. A mosque will have its own special holiness attached to it. Such as when the faithful believers said: We shall build a mosque where the people of the cave, who left the comforts and convenience of city dwelling and escaped to seek refuge in the harsh desert and cave, in their honour.

{لَنَتَّخِذَنَّ عَلَيْهِم مَّسْجِدًا}

'We will raise over them a place of worship.' (Al Kahf 18:21)

3. The first thing the Prophetﷺ did after migration was the building of a mosque.

$$\{لَمَسْجِدٌ أُسِّسَ عَلَى التَّقْوَىٰ مِنْ أَوَّلِ يَوْمٍ\}$$

A mosque that was founded upon god fearing from the first day. (Al Tawba 9:108)

4. More than ten times, the name of the The Holy Mosque[1] has been mentioned in the Holy Qur'ān.

5. Allahﷻ recognises a mosque as His Own House and the best of people, in other words Prophetﷺ Ibrahīm﷿ and Ismail ﷿, two significant Prophets, are appointed as its servants.

$$\{طَهِّرَا بَيْتِيَ\}$$

Purify My House (Al Baqarah 2:125)

6. For the purposes of attending a mosque, it has been advised to dress with adornments and beauty (clean/new and ironed clothes).

$$\{خُذُوا زِينَتَكُمْ عِندَ كُلِّ مَسْجِدٍ\}$$

Take your adornment at every place of worship.
(Al A'rāf 7:31).

7. If a mosque is built with anything other than with the intention of God and obedience, and it becomes a place where the seeds of disunity is sown, then it must be dismantled.

$$\{مَسْجِدًا ضِرَارًا وَكُفْرًا وَتَفْرِيقًا بَيْنَ الْمُؤْمِنِينَ\}$$

A mosque in opposition and unbelief, and to divide the believers (Tawbah 9:107)

8. The holiness of a mosque is so much so that not just any one can go around building and improving a mosque!

---

[1] المسجد الحرام is mentioned fifteen times.

{مَا كَانَ لِلْمُشْرِكِينَ أَن يَعْمُرُوا مَسَاجِدَ اللَّـهِ}

It is not for the idolaters to maintain God's places of worship. (Tawbah 9:17).

And this issue is specific to God wary and brave believers, whom other than Allah۩, are afraid of no one else.

{إِنَّمَا يَعْمُرُ مَسَاجِدَ اللَّهِ مَنْ آمَنَ بِاللَّهِ وَالْيَوْمِ الْآخِرِ وَأَقَامَ الصَّلَاةَ وَآتَى الزَّكَاةَ وَلَمْ يَخْشَ إِلَّا اللَّهَ}

Only he shall inhabit God's places of worship who believes in God and the Last Day, and performs the prayer, and pays the alms, and fears none but God alone.

(Tawbah 9:18)

9. Mosques and the rest of the places for the worship of God of Heavenly religions such as Christianity and Judaism (churches and synagogues) are of such value that their protection demands the self-sacrifice.

{لَّهُدِّمَتْ صَوَامِعُ وَبِيَعٌ وَصَلَوَاتٌ}

There had been destroyed cloisters and churches, oratories and mosques (Al Hajj 22:40).

Should Allah۩ not allow the brave and revolutionary to prevent unfaithful entering places of worship, every place of worship would be destroyed.

10. The Mosque, and the presence of one in it has its own manners and conditions attached, some of which include not raising one's voice, speaking nonsense, not talking about buying and selling merchandise, or go chasing worldly idle conversations.

11. Each step towards a Mosque has its own reward.

12. Sitting in the Mosque in anticipation for the time of Prayers, has its own reward.

13. A Mosque that does not hold prayers, will complain to Allah۩.

14. The home prayer of one who neighbours a Mosque has no value.[1]
15. For the sake of those who are Mosque goers, Allahﷻ will remove the punishment of others.

In narrations, we find that it is stated one who visits and returns from a Mosque often, has many benefits attributed to them, such as: Finding their religious friend and brother, gains beneficial awareness, guidance and separation from sin, coming across Divine Blessings and Mercy. The Prophetﷺ stated: "Simply seeing someone attending a Mosque brings about their awareness of their own faith."

Maintenance And Prosperity

{إِنَّمَا يَعْمُرُ مَسَاجِدَ اللَّـهِ مَنْ آمَنَ بِاللَّـهِ وَالْيَوْمِ الْآخِرِ وَأَقَامَ الصَّلَاةَ وَآتَى الزَّكَاةَ وَلَمْ يَخْشَ إِلَّا اللَّـهَ فَعَسَىٰ أُولَـٰئِكَ أَن يَكُونُوا مِنَ الْمُهْتَدِينَ}

Only he shall inhabit God's places of worship who believes in God and the Last

Day, and performs the prayer, and pays the alms, and fears none but God alone; it

may be that those will be among the guided. (Tawbah 9:18).

The Mosque is an important foundation of worship and society of Muslims. Therefore, not only do the custodians of the Mosque need to be pious and pure, their program be for growth and cultivation, their budget appropriately and jurisprudentially pure, but also the Mosque goers be people of piety and be with Allahﷻ and be people of respect. Otherwise, if those who build Mosques are tyrants, monarchs, liturgists, be uneducated, fearful and their servants also lazy and overly relaxed, of course Mosques will lose their original intention of being for spiritual prosperity and will remain far from that intention.

Adornments and The Mosque

{يَا بَنِي آدَمَ خُذُوا زِينَتَكُمْ عِندَ كُلِّ مَسْجِدٍ وَكُلُوا وَاشْرَبُوا وَلَا تُسْرِفُوا إِنَّهُ لَا يُحِبُّ الْمُسْرِفِينَ}

Children of Adam! Take your adornment at every place of worship; and eat and

drink but be you not prodigal; He loves not the prodigal. (Al A'rāf 7:31)

---

[1] Translators Comment: There are conditions associated to this such as inability due to valid excuse (for example illness).

It could be said: When the Holy Qur'ān speaks to the "Children of Adam", He is addressing all of mankind of all religions and such like.

Holy Qur'ān refers to offspring and wealth as adornments:

$$\{لْمَالُ وَالْبَنُونَ زِينَةُ الْحَيَاةِ الدُّنْيَا\}$$
Wealth and sons are the adornment of the present world;
(Al Kahf 18:46).

So, it could be also concluded that the Ayah (7:31) is suggesting that when we go to the Mosque, we also take along our children and wealth, so that with the wealth, we solve the economic problems of the Islamic society and so that with our children, among Mosques and the Islamic society, problems with upbringing of the future generation is resolved.

In narrations, a just Imam of the Mosque, visible adornments, wearing perfume and presentable clothing during prayers, raising the hands during prayers, joining the congregational prayers of Eid (After the Holy month of Ramadhān and after pilgrimage), Friday prayers, are all considered to be part of the realities of adornments.

Imam Hasan A.S while in prayers and inside mosques, would wear the best of clothing and state "For certainly Allah is Beautiful and He loves beauty, so I beautify myself for my Lord", and would then recite the Ayah mentioned.

Allah loves beauty and adornments, for if He did not, he would not have ordered as such - "Take your adornment" – and as Islam is the intuitive religion, and mankind intuitively and naturally loves beauty.

With regards to adornments while going to mosques, it is respect towards the worshippers, to worshipping, and is also a cause for practically attracting and encouraging others to attend mosques. For otherwise, the use of adornments and food to attract is natural and intuitive, but under certain conditions such as the presence of the poor and needy, there must be sympathy and empathy towards them. Therefore, we read in the narrations that there was a difference in the clothing of Imam Sādiq, where the people were living in comfort, as opposed to the society in which Imam Ali resided over, where the community was a poorer community.

With a little attention to the Ayah, there are several points we can extract, some of which are:

1. The mosque, which is a foundation of the Islamic society, must be adorned, beautiful, and be attractive.
2. The best and most beautiful clothing must be for the best of places.
3. Islam heeds not only the inner and heart felt attention towards prayers[1], but also towards the outer appearance. Yes, the inner and outer, the worldly and hereafter affairs, are all interlinked in Islam.
4. Adornments during prayers performed singularly are also important, but adornments in congregational prayers has special features.
5. First prayers, then food. The Ayah brings our attention to spiritual nutrition (prayers) before the bodily nutrition (food).

---

[1] Al Muiminūn 23:2

Lesson 28 Etiquettes of Society

Our Selection of Friends

{وَيَوْمَ يَعَضُّ الظَّالِمُ عَلَىٰ يَدَيْهِ يَقُولُ يَا لَيْتَنِي اتَّخَذْتُ مَعَ الرَّسُولِ سَبِيلًا يَا وَيْلَتَىٰ لَيْتَنِي لَمْ أَتَّخِذْ فُلَانًا خَلِيلًا لَّقَدْ أَضَلَّنِي عَنِ الذِّكْرِ بَعْدَ إِذْ جَاءَنِي وَكَانَ الشَّيْطَانُ لِلْإِنسَانِ خَذُولًا}

Upon the day the evildoer shall bite his hands, saying, 'Would that I had taken a way along with the Messenger!, Alas, would that I had not taken So-and-so for a friend! He indeed led me astray from the Remembrance, after it had come to me; Satan is ever a forsaker of men.' (Al Furqān 25:27-29).

Islam has advised us plentifully on many facets of friendship – selecting friends, how to know them, the parameters and borders of friendship, etiquettes of socialising and their rights. It is encouraged to befriend certain individuals, whereas it is prohibited to befriend others. Some of these advices are listed below:

- If you are in doubt with regards to an individual as to whether you should befriend them or not, look at their friends to find out more about them

فانضروا الى خُلَطائه[1]

---

[1] (Bihar Al Anwar بحار الأنوار) V74 P197

- Being alone is better than befriending a bad person.
- The Prophet was asked – Who is the best of friends? To which he replied: One who, when you see them reminds you of Allah, and with what they say, increases your knowledge, and by their actions, are reminded of Resurrection Day.
- Imam Ali states that it is when you lose your abilities that you can distinguish your true friends from your enemies.
- Imam Ali states a good friend is the best family.
- In narrations, it has been said that true friendships are tested with anger, money, and travel. If the friendship survives these tests, it is a true one.

Brotherhood

{إِنَّمَا الْمُؤْمِنُونَ إِخْوَةٌ فَأَصْلِحُوا بَيْنَ أَخَوَيْكُمْ
وَاتَّقُوا اللَّـهَ لَعَلَّكُمْ تُرْحَمُونَ}

The believers indeed are brothers; so set things right between your two brothers,

and fear God; haply so you will find mercy. (Al Hujurāt 49:10).

One of the features of Islam is that reconciliation starts at the roots of faith. For example, in this Ayah, for reconciliation, the etiquette of an individual and society must be based upon intellectually and foundations of faith. All the faithful are brothers, so why the arguments and ill-feelings?

The utilisation of brotherhood is an innovation of Islamic teachings.

At the beginning of Islam, the Prophet along with seven hundred and forty people were at a place called "*Nakhila*", when Archangel Jibraīl descended and stated that Allah has formed contracts of brotherhood between angels, and the Prophet also formed brotherhood relations between his companions in which each individual became the brother of the other – Abu Bakr with Omar, Salman with Abu Dhar, Talha with Zubair, Miqdād with Ammar, A'isha with Hafsa, Um Salma with Saffiya, and the Prophet himself with Imam Ali .[1]

The term brotherhood is not limited to that of the male gender, but also encompasses women -

---

[1] (Bihar Al Anwar بحار الأنوار) V38 P335

{وَإِن كَانُوا إِخْوَةً رِّجَالًا وَنِسَاءً}

And if they are brothers, men or women (Al Nisā 4:176).

What is more important than getting a brother is the protection of the brotherhood. In the narrations, those who dump brotherly relations are strongly condemned, and the advice is that if your brother in faith leaves you, that you should approach and visit them –

صل من قطعك[1]

Imam Sādiq ﷺ states that the true believer is the brother of a true believer, so much so they are like one body, if a part of the body becomes ill, the whole body becomes uncomfortable.

The Rights of Our Brothers

The Prophet ﷺ stated that upon brothers in faith have thirty rights which are expected and demanded of each other, they are:

1. Forgiveness and mercy
2. Keeping each other's secrets
3. Compensating for their errors
4. Accepting their excuse
5. Protecting them from the ill intended
6. Wanting the best for each other
7. Keeping promises
8. Visiting one who is ill
9. Attending their funeral
10. Accepting their invitations and gifts
11. Rewarding in return for gifts
12. Thanking them for their services
13. Strive to help
14. Protecting their honour
15. Attending to their needs
16. Be the means of resolving their problems
17. Guiding them when lost
18. Blessing them when they sneeze
19. Answer their greetings (Salam)

---

[1] (Bihar Al Anwar بحار الأنوار) V78 P71

20. Respecting their words
21. Preparing their gift in a good manner
22. Accepting their oath
23. Befriending their friends and not be their enemy
24. Not leaving them where an unfortunate event occurs
25. Anything they want for themselves, should be wanted for them

Reconciliation and Peace

Islam looks towards a peaceful and reconciliatory life, one of the Divine blessings that is in the Holy Qur'ān, is the affection in the hearts of Muslims. This can be seen in this Ayah:

{إِذْ كُنتُمْ أَعْدَاءً فَأَلَّفَ بَيْنَ قُلُوبِكُمْ}

Remember God's blessing upon you when you were enemies, and He brought your hearts together. (Āle Imrān 3:10).

Reconciliation is a reason for the granting of mercy and forgiveness from Allah:

{وَإِن تُصْلِحُوا وَتَتَّقُوا فَإِنَّ اللَّـهَ كَانَ غَفُورًا رَّحِيمًا}

If you set things right, and are godfearing, God is All-forgiving, All-compassionate. (An Nisā 4:129).

And whomever intervenes to assist in reconciliation will be the subject of reward themselves:

{مَّن يَشْفَعْ شَفَاعَةً حَسَنَةً يَكُن لَّهُ نَصِيبٌ مِّنْهَا}

Whoso intercedes with a good intercession shall receive a share of it (An Nisā 4:85).

Islam has specified certain rulings with regards to reconciliation between people, such as:

1. Lying is considered a greater sin, however, if utilised for reconciliation will not be considered a sin nor is it punishable.

لا كذب على المصلح

2. Whispering and speaking softly in to the ear is a satanic deed and is not recommended in Islam, but if it is for reconciliation is not prohibited.

لا خير في كثير من نجواهم الا من امر بصدقة او معروف

او اصلاح بين الناس

3. Acting upon an oath is obligatory and reneging on an oath is considered a sin and prohibited, but this is forgone if one swears to never reconcile between two people.[1] Although the execution of the will of the deceased is obligatory, if one fears it will cause sedition between people it is recommended to withhold executing the will until there is reconciliation between the affected parties[2].

Religious Connections and Relationships

In the twenty first Ayah of Surah Ar Rād, as an indication of the wisdom, Allah discusses those who have a relationship with what He has ordered.

{وَالَّذِينَ يَصِلُونَ مَا أَمَرَ اللَّـهُ بِهِ أَن يُوصَلَ}

Who join what God has commanded shall be joined. (Ar Rād 13:21).

And in narrations we have that what Allah has ordered for a strong connection is the familial relationship, meaning the guarding and protection of the strong interfamily relationships as well as the strong link with the Guardian and Divine Leadership and to proactively support the line of Guardianship.[3]

Relationships which Allah has ordered strong links with include:

1. Cultural links to academics.[4]
2. Social links to the people.[5]
3. Affectionate relationship with the parents.[6]

---

[1] Surah Al-Baqarah 2:224

[2] Surah Al-Baqarah 2:182

[3] (Tafsir Safi تفسير الصافي)

[4] Holy Quran 16:43, 21:7

[5] Holy Quran 3:200

[6] Holy Quran 2:83, 4:36, 6:151, 17:23, 46:15

4. Financial links with those in need.[1]
5. Intellectual links with in social circles.[2]
6. Political links to the Guardians.[3]
7. All forms of relationships with believers.[4]
8. Spiritual relationships with religious role models.[5]

---

[1] Holy Quran 2:245, 57:11
[2] Holy Quran 3:159
[3] Holy Quran 4:59
[4] Holy Quran 49:10
[5] Holy Quran 33:21

Lesson 29 Family

Responsibilities of Society in Marrying the Youth

{وَأَنكِحُوا الْأَيَامَىٰ مِنكُمْ وَالصَّالِحِينَ مِنْ عِبَادِكُمْ وَإِمَائِكُمْ إِن يَكُونُوا فُقَرَاءَ يُغْنِهِمُ اللَّـهُ مِن فَضْلِهِ وَاللَّـهُ وَاسِعٌ عَلِيمٌ}

Marry the spouseless among you, and your slaves and handmaidens that are righteous; if they are poor, God will enrich them of His bounty; God is All-embracing, All-knowing. (An Nūr 24:32).

The spouseless in the Ayah refers to all who have no spouses, be it male or female, a widow or one who has never married before.

Marriage in Islam is a sacred issue and is a matter of emphasis, and the family and society are responsible for marrying those who are without a spouse, and there is no need for prescribing who should ask who in marriage, with both sides of the potential relationship able to make the first approach. Of course, Allah has secured the blessings of the bride and grooms lives in a Divine Decree and marriage is a means to increased blessings and scope in life.

Islam recognises marriage as sacred, in contrast to Christians who see that celibacy as the more valued path and so the Pope and Priests must not marry.

In narrations, we read that marriage is protection of half of one's religion, and a two rakaat prayer[1] of one who is married is worth seventy times more than one who is single. The sleep of one who is married is better than the fasting of one who is single while awake.

In contrast to the beliefs that marriage brings upon poverty, the Prophetﷺ stated that marriage increases ones' sustenance. Imam Sādiq ؏ also says that embitterment of one's life is under the shadow of marriage. They also state that one who leaves marriage due to being fearful of the financial distress of marriage is not of us and has ill-doubts about Allah.

Marriage is a means to comfort[2]. In marriage, families become closer and hearts become merciful, and the grounds for the upbringing of a new, pure generation and spirit of collaboration is founded.

The parents who stand in the way of their children's marriage are partners in the sins of their children should these sins be a result of not getting married.

In narrations, we read that we should hasten the marriage of our children, and our daughters that reach the age of marriage is like a fruit that has ripened that if not picked from the tree at the appropriate time will become decayed.[3]

The best intermediary is intercession, and intermediation is a component of marriage, as our narrations state: One who secures a marriage for the bride or groom is in the shadow of The Throne of Allah.

We also read in the narrations that one who acts in the way of marrying his brother in religion will be subject to the Divine Favour for Allah on the Day of Resurrection.

Of course, the Ayah after says:

{وَلْيَسْتَعْفِفِ الَّذِينَ لَا يَجِدُونَ نِكَاحًا حَتَّىٰ يُغْنِيَهُمُ اللَّـهُ مِن فَضْلِهِ}

And let those who find not the means to marry be abstinent till God enriches them of His bounty. (An Nūr 24:33).

---

[1] A short form of prayer which has two prostrations.
[2] Holy Quran 30:21
[3] (Mizan Al-Hikmah ميزان الحِكمة)

Both family and government ("Marry the spouseless") and the wealthy of the society are to assist ("God will enrich them of His bounty").

Of course, in the process of choosing a spouse, one must be careful not to allow emotion take over. Do not rush, and only after thorough deliberation, advice and discussion should one proceed. Many of the issues that arise within marriages are a result of a lack of due diligence in the choice one makes of their spouse. The spouse is your partner in life and their influence will be for the rest of one's life and until the Day of Resurrection. Most of the shallow marriages that result from chance and one-off encounters, or acquainted on the bus or in a park, don't end up well.

Kinds of Families in The Holy Qur'ān

The Holy Qur'ān has presented us with four types of families:

1. A husband and wife that are on the same par with regards to their beliefs and synchronous with their pious deeds. (Like Imam Ali ؏ and Sayyida Fātima ؏ are role models of a partnership where faith and deed were in sync, and the Ayāt in Surah Dahr point to how night after night they gave their food for breaking their fast to the poor, orphan and slave).[1]
2. A husband and wife that are on the same par with regards to their evil thoughts and deeds. (Such as that with Abu Lahab and his wife, despite being the uncle of the Prophet؍ on the fathers' side, were abusive towards the Prophet؍ and did their best to break the Dawn of Islam. The wife of Abu Lahab would throw firewood upon the Prophet؍ to hurt and bother him).[2]
3. A family in which the male is pious, but the wife is evil (such as in the example of Prophet Lot؏ and Prophet Noah؏).[3]
4. A family in which the wife is pious, but the husband is evil (Such as in the example of Pharaoh and his wife).[4]

Responsibilities Within the Family

In various Ayāt of the Holy Qur'ān, duties towards one's family are indicated:

---

[1] Holy Quran 76:8
[2] Holy Quran 111: 1-5
[3] Holy Quran 66:10
[4] Holy Quran 66:11

- Protect yourself and your family from the fire of Hell.[1]
- Bid your family towards prayers and make be patient it.[2]
- Advise your closest of relatives (towards piety).[3]
- Advice your children to perform prayers and enjoin good.[4]
- Spiritual people have an inclination towards their families and are not indifferent.[5]
- The Prophetﷺ would advise his own family to perform prayers.[6]

In narrations, we also notice considerable attention to this subject:

- The Prophetﷺ would state that everyone of us is responsible for those under your care, the husband over the family and the wife over the husband and children.[7]
- Imam Ali ؏ states: Teach yourselves and family goodness and give them manners.[8]

---

[1] Holy Quran 66:6
[2] Holy Quran 20:132
[3] Holy Quran 26:214
[4] Holy Quran 31:17
[5] Holy Quran 52:26
[6] Holy Quran 19:55
[7] (Majmaat Warram مجموعة ورّام) V1 P6
[8] (Muniyat Al Mareed منية المريد) P380

Lesson 30 The Festivities of The Liberated

The Liberated in The Qur'ān

{قَدْ أَفْلَحَ الْمُؤْمِنُونَ

الَّذِينَ هُمْ فِي صَلَاتِهِمْ خَاشِعُونَ}

Prosperous are the believers who in their prayers are humble. (Al Muminūn 23:1-2).

In the Holy Qur'ān, those individuals and groups who succeed and prosper have been identified, as those who:

- Serve Allah

{وَاعْبُدُوا رَبَّكُمْ وَافْعَلُوا الْخَيْرَ لَعَلَّكُمْ تُفْلِحُونَ}

And serve your Lord, and do good; haply so you shall prosper; (Al Hajj22:77)

- Do deeds and work that is valuable

{فَمَن ثَقُلَتْ مَوَازِينُهُ فَأُولَـٰئِكَ هُمُ الْمُفْلِحُونَ}

Then he whose scales are heavy - they are the prosperous, (Al Mu'minūn 23:102).

- Are not stingy

{وَمَن يُوقَ شُحَّ نَفْسِهِ فَأُولَـٰئِكَ هُمُ الْمُفْلِحُونَ}

And whoso is guarded against the avarice of his own soul, those -- they are the prosperous. (Al- Hashr 59:9).

- Are with Allah

{أَلَا إِنَّ حِزْبَ اللَّـهِ هُمُ الْمُفْلِحُونَ}

Why, surely God's party -- they are the prosperous. (Al-Mujadala 58:22).

- Are people of Remembrance

{وَاذْكُرُوا اللَّـهَ كَثِيرًا لَعَلَّكُمْ تُفْلِحُونَ}

and remember God frequently; haply so you will prosper.
(Al-Anfal 8:45)

- Are God wary

{فَاتَّقُوا اللَّـهَ يَا أُولِي الْأَلْبَابِ لَعَلَّكُمْ تُفْلِحُونَ}

So fear God, O men possessed of minds; haply so you will prosper. (Al-Ma'ida 5:100).

- Are strugglers

{وَجَاهِدُوا فِي سَبِيلِهِ لَعَلَّكُمْ تُفْلِحُونَ}

And struggle in His way; haply you will prosper. (Al-Ma'ida 5:35).

- Who repent

{وَتُوبُوا إِلَى اللَّـهِ جَمِيعًا أَيُّهَ الْمُؤْمِنُونَ لَعَلَّكُمْ تُفْلِحُونَ}

And turn all together to God (in repentance), O you believers; haply so you will prosper. (An-Nur 24:31)

Ramadhān Eid: A Reward from Allah

Imam Baqir stated that the Prophet said: Whenever the first day of the month of Shawwal arrives[1], a caller will call out "Oh you who believe! Rush

---

[1] The day after the last day of the Holy Month of Ramadhān, or "Eid Al-Fitr".

towards your rewards". At that point, the Imam turns to Jaber and states: Oh Jaber, the prizes from Allah are not like the prizes from these kings. Today, is the day of (Divine) prizes.

Imam Hasan came across people who were laughing and playing on the day of Eid Al-Fitr and said to his companions: Allah made the Month of Ramdhan a field for competition and access to His Mercy and Pleasure that some have taken this opportunity, while others fell behind and lost. Amazed am I of those who in the wake of this day of reward, those who are pre-occupied with play and laughter.

Imam Riḍha states: Allah has made the day of "Fitr" a reason to celebrate, so that Muslims can congregate and come together on this day and be able to praise and glorify Allah for His favours and blessings upon them, and to pay their religious taxes (Zakāt and Fitriyah), to relish and venerate Allah.

From this narration, the philosophy of this day and the prayer of this great day can be summarised in the following points:

1. A day of congregation and assembly
2. To pay the Ramadhān Charity[1] and give attention to the poor
3. To gravitate towards and relish Allah
4. Supplication and beseech Allah at His doorstep.

Remembering The Resurrection

Some of the developmental effects of the Eid Prayers on this day is that the presence of the needy amongst the congregation in a place of worship without a roof, people are reminded of Allah and the Day of Resurrection and their own needs for the Mercy of Allah, and the image of something similar to the Day of Resurrection can be visualised.

Imam Ali in a speech that he said on a day that was Eid Al Fitr, he said to the people – Oh People, this is your day, so that those righteous receive their reward. On this day, the wicked will be at a loss, this day is the closest day to you to your Day of Resurrection.

The coming out of your homes to the mosques is a reminder of you coming out of your graves. By your waiting for the prayer to start in the places of worship, you will be reminded of your waiting for Allah in the Resurrection.

---

[1] Referred to as Zakāt.

And your return to your homes will be the reminder of your return to your homes in Paradise, or Hell.

In the prescribed supplication of this prayer, we become aware and are reminded of the Greatness, Might, Forgiveness, Mercy and Pardon of Allah, and we seek from Him in honour and respect of this great day, that is the festival of Muslims and source of honour and pride for the Prophet and his Purified Household, that You (oh Allah) bless Mohammad and his Purified Household and that you allow us to benefit from his goodness and blessings.

Part of this supplication includes the most comprehensive requests one could ask for, it is that: *I seek from you Oh Allah, that you enter me in to every goodness with which You entered Mohammad and his Purified Household, and that You save me from every evil you saved Mohammad and his Purified Household. Oh Allah, I ask for the best of which your righteous servants ask for, and seek your refuge from everything that your righteous servants have sought your refuge from.*

Remembering Those Before Us

One of the traditions of this day that is popular amongst Muslims is the remembering of those who have been laid to rest and celebrating them. The Prophet stated:

زُرِ القُبُورَ تُذَكِّرُ بِهَا الآخِرَةَ

Visit the graves and remember with it the Hereafter.

He also stated that whoever visits the graves of their parents or similar every Friday, not only will their sins be forgiven but also be considered amongst the righteous children.

We also read: Supplications recited near the tombs of parents are answered.

Imam Riḍha states that if while visiting the tomb of a believer, Surah Al Qadr is recited seven times, both the deceased and their visitor will be the subject of Divine Forgiveness and Pardon. In narrations, it is also stated that the deceased are aware of and become happy when you visit them and become fond of you.

And All Praise Is To Allah The Sustainer Of The World